The Learning Age

a renaissance for a new Britain

Presented to Parliament by
the Secretary of State for Education and Employment
by Command of Her Majesty

February 1998

Cm 3790

£9.40

Contents

England, Scotland, Wales and Northern Ireland

Many of the issues covered in this consultation paper are relevant across the UK. This paper covers specific proposals for England. The Secretaries of State for Scotland, Wales and Northern Ireland are responsible for education and training policy in these parts of the UK. The Secretaries of State for Scotland and for Wales plan to issue their own documents on lifelong learning in these countries, including how the University for Industry will be taken forward. In Northern Ireland Ministers will undertake a consultative process on the issues raised.

Foreword by the Secretary of State

Learning is the key to prosperity - for each of us as individuals, as well as for the nation as a whole. Investment in human capital will be the foundation of success in the knowledge-based global economy of the twenty-first century. This is why the Government has put learning at the heart of its ambition. Our first policy paper addressed school standards. This Green Paper sets out for consultation how learning throughout life will build human capital by encouraging the acquisition of knowledge and skills and emphasising creativity and imagination. The fostering of an enquiring mind and the love of learning are essential to our future success.

To achieve stable and sustainable growth, we will need a well-educated, well-equipped and adaptable labour force. To cope with rapid change and the challenge of the information and communication age, we must ensure that people can return to learning throughout their lives. We cannot rely on a small elite, no matter how highly educated or highly paid. Instead, we need the creativity, enterprise and scholarship of all our people.

As well as securing our economic future, learning has a wider contribution. It helps make ours a civilised society, develops the spiritual side of our lives and promotes active citizenship. Learning enables people to play a full part in their community. It strengthens the family, the neighbourhood and consequently the nation. It helps us fulfil our potential and opens doors to a love of music, art and literature. That is why we value learning for its own sake as well as for the equality of opportunity it brings.

To realise our ambition, we must all develop and sustain a regard for learning at whatever age. For many people this will mean overcoming past experiences which have put them off learning. For others it will mean taking the opportunity, perhaps for the first time, to recognise their own talent, to discover new ways of learning and to see new opportunities opening up. What was previously available only to the few can, in the century ahead, be something which is enjoyed and taken advantage of by the many.

That is why this Green Paper encourages adults to enter and re-enter learning at every point in their lives, whatever their experience at school. There are many ways in which we can all take advantage of new opportunities:

- as parents we can play our part in encouraging, supporting and raising the expectations of our children by learning alongside them;

- as members of the workforce we can take on the challenge of learning in and out of work; and

- as citizens we can balance the rights we can expect from the state, with the responsibilities of individuals for their own future, sharing the gains and the investment needed.

Two initiatives will exemplify our approach:

- individual learning accounts which will enable men and women to take responsibility for their own learning with support from both Government and employers; and

- the University for Industry which will offer access to a learning network to help people deepen their knowledge, update their skills and gain new ones.

We are fortunate in this country to have a great tradition of learning. We have inherited the legacy of the great self-help movements of the Victorian industrial communities. Men and women, frequently living in desperate poverty, were determined to improve themselves and their families. They did so through the creation of libraries, study at workers' institutes, through the pioneering efforts of the early trade unions, at evening classes, through public lectures and by correspondence courses. Learning enriched their lives and they, in turn, enriched the whole of society.

The Learning Age will be built on a renewed commitment to self-improvement and on a recognition of the enormous contribution learning makes to our society. Learning helps shape the values which we pass on to each succeeding generation. Learning supports active citizenship and democracy, giving men and women the capacity to provide leadership in their communities. As President John F Kennedy once put it: "Liberty without learning is always in peril and learning without liberty is always in vain".

This Green Paper is the start of a consultation process which will help shape the Learning Age. I invite you to offer your views and to make your contribution to ensuring that the United Kingdom is working, and is working for everyone, in the first crucial decade of a new millennium.

David Blunkett
Secretary of State for Education and Employment

"Education is the best economic policy we have."

Rt Hon Tony Blair MP

Introduction

The Learning Age

1. We are in a new age - the age of information and of global competition. Familiar certainties and old ways of doing things are disappearing. The types of jobs we do have changed as have the industries in which we work and the skills they need. At the same time, new opportunities are opening up as we see the potential of new technologies to change our lives for the better. We have no choice but to prepare for this new age in which the key to success will be the continuous education and development of the human mind and imagination.

2. Over a generation we have seen a fundamental change in the balance between skilled and unskilled jobs in the industrialised world. Since the 1960s, employment in manufacturing has fallen from one in three of the workforce to under one in five. This has been mirrored by a huge rise in jobs in services which now account for over two-thirds of all workers; more people today work in film and television than in car manufacturing. There are three million self-employed and 6.5 million part-time workers, and women make up nearly half the workforce compared with less than a third 50 years ago.

3. The Industrial Revolution was built on capital investment in plant and machinery, skills and hard physical labour. British inventors pushed forward the frontiers of technology and our manufacturers turned their inventions into wealth. We built the world's first calculator, jet engine, computer and television. Our history shows what we are capable of, but we must now apply the same qualities of skill and invention to a fresh challenge.

4. The information and knowledge-based revolution of the twenty-first century will be built on a very different foundation - investment in the intellect and creativity of people. The microchip and fibre optic cable are today what electricity and the steam engine were to the nineteenth century. The United Kingdom is also pioneering this new age, combining ingenuity, enterprise, design and marketing skills. We are world leaders in information and communication technologies and bio-technology.

5. To continue to compete, we must equip ourselves to cope with the enormous economic and social change we face, to make sense of the rapid transformation of the world, and to encourage imagination and innovation. We will succeed by transforming inventions into new wealth, just as we did a hundred years ago. But unlike then, *everyone* must have the opportunity to innovate and to gain reward - not just in research laboratories, but on the production line, in design studios, in retail outlets, and in providing services.

6. The most productive investment will be linked to the best educated and best trained workforces, and the most effective way of getting and keeping a job will be to have the skills needed by employers.

7. Our single greatest challenge is to equip ourselves for this new age with new and better skills, with knowledge and with understanding.

Learning's potential

8. Our vision of the Learning Age is about more than employment. The development of a culture of learning will help to build a united society, assist in the creation of personal independence, and encourage our creativity and innovation. Learning encompasses basic literacy to advanced scholarship. We learn in many different ways through formal study, reading, watching television, going on a training course, taking an evening class, at work, and from family and friends. In this consultation paper we use the word 'learning' to describe all of these.

9. This country has a great learning tradition. We have superb universities and colleges which help maintain our position as a world leader in technology, finance, design, manufacturing and the creative industries. We want more people to have the chance to experience the richness of this tradition by participating in learning. We want all to benefit from the opportunities learning brings and to make them more widely available by building on this foundation of high standards and excellence.

10. For *individuals*:

- learning offers excitement and the opportunity for discovery. It stimulates enquiring minds and nourishes our souls. It takes us in directions we never expected, sometimes changing our lives. Learning helps create and sustain our culture. It helps all of us to improve our chances of getting a job and of getting on. Learning increases our earning power, helps older people to stay healthy and active, strengthens families and the wider community, and encourages independence. There are many people for whom learning has opened up, for the first time in their lives, the chance to explore art, music, literature, film, and the theatre, or to become creative themselves. Learning has enabled many people to help others to experience these joys too.

11. For *businesses*:

- learning helps them to be more successful by adding value and keeping them up-to-date. Learning develops the intellectual capital which is now at the centre of a nation's competitive strength. It provides the tools to manage industrial and technological change, and helps generate ideas, research and innovation. Because productivity depends on the whole workforce, we must invest in everyone.

12. For *communities:*

- learning contributes to social cohesion and fosters a sense of belonging, responsibility and identity. In communities affected by rapid economic change and industrial restructuring, learning builds local capacity to respond to this change.

13. For *the nation:*

- learning is essential to a strong economy and an inclusive society. In offering a way out of dependency and low expectation, it lies at the heart of the Government's welfare reform programme. We must bridge the 'learning divide' - between those who have benefited from education and training and those who have not - which blights so many communities and widens income inequality. The results are seen in the second and third generation of the same family being unemployed, and in the potential talent of young people wasted in a vicious circle of under-achievement, self-deprecation, and petty crime. Learning can overcome this by building self-confidence and independence.

The purpose of this consultation paper

14. This consultation paper has five main purposes. It is intended to begin both a national debate and a process of change which the Government expects to continue throughout the lifetime of this Parliament and beyond.

15. First, the consultation paper sets out *why* this country urgently needs a new strategy for lifelong learning. It argues that this is essential if our people, businesses and the nation are to respond to the challenges and opportunities which now face them.

16. Secondly, the paper explains *what is meant* by lifelong learning in all its rich variety and diversity. Lifelong learning means the continuous development of the skills, knowledge and understanding that are essential for employability and fulfilment.

17. Thirdly, the paper describes *who* is currently involved in learning and, more importantly, who needs to be drawn into learning in future. Increasing demand for learning - and responding to it with imagination and high standards - will be a major challenge.

18. Fourthly, the paper outlines *how* the Government intends to carry forward its strategy for lifelong learning through a number of initiatives. Some of these have already been announced; others are in their development stage. They include 500,000 additional people in further and higher education, the New Deal for the young and long-term unemployed, the University for Industry (UfI), individual learning accounts and the National Grid for Learning.

19. Finally, the paper is intended to stimulate responses and ideas from individuals and organisations. These will be invaluable in helping us to shape our plans for the Learning Age.

20. In preparing this consultation paper, we have drawn on many sources. These include, in particular, the reports produced by the following groups:

- the Committee on Widening Participation set up by the Further Education Funding Council (FEFC) and chaired by Helena Kennedy QC (now Baroness Kennedy);

- the committees on 16-19 qualifications and on higher education chaired by Sir Ron (now Lord) Dearing;

- the National Advisory Group for Continuing Education and Lifelong Learning chaired by Professor Bob Fryer; and

- the University for Industry Design and Implementation Advisory Group chaired by David Brown of Motorola Ltd.

The scale of the challenge

21. The country's current learning 'scoreboard' shows strengths, but also some serious weaknesses. A great strength is our universities which educate to degree and postgraduate level and set world-class standards. The UK is second only to the USA in the number of major scientific prizes awarded in the last five years. The proportion of graduates in the working population has almost doubled over a decade. Our research excellence is valued by many companies which choose to base their research capacity in the UK. A further strength is the existing commitment among many people to gaining qualifications. Fourteen million people have National Vocational Qualification (NVQ) level 2 (equivalent to five or more higher grade GCSEs).

22. Our weakness lies in our performance in basic and intermediate skills. Almost 30 per cent of young people fail to reach NVQ level 2 by the age of 19. Seven million adults have no formal qualifications at all; 21 million adults have not reached level 3 (equivalent to 2 A levels), and more than one in five of all adults have poor literacy and numeracy skills. As the chart below shows, we lag behind France, Germany, the USA and Singapore in the proportion of our workforce qualified to level 3. In the case of graduates, even though we have a high number, we need to encourage more of our highly qualified people to update their skills through continuing professional development.

Proportion of the working population qualified to a given level

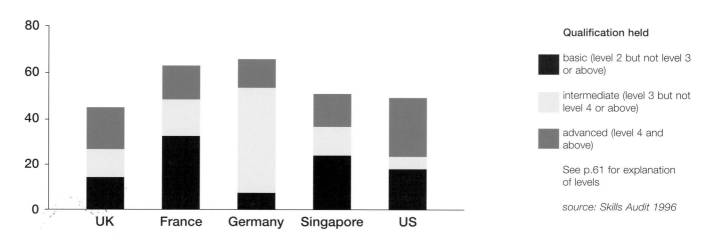

Qualification held

■ basic (level 2 but not level 3 or above)

□ intermediate (level 3 but not level 4 or above)

■ advanced (level 4 and above)

See p.61 for explanation of levels

source: Skills Audit 1996

Principles

23. Meeting this challenge will require a quiet and sustained revolution in aspiration and achievement. It will begin with getting the foundations right in the home and at school. Our White Paper *Excellence in Schools* (Cm 3681) (The Stationery Office, 1997) has begun this process, but we need to carry it forward throughout life. It will mean changing the culture in many homes and workplaces where learning is not seen as having any relevance. It is a social as well as an economic challenge.

24. The Government's role will be to help create a framework of opportunities for people to learn and to lift barriers that prevent them from taking up those opportunities. We cannot force anyone to learn - individuals must take that responsibility themselves - but we can help those who want to develop a thirst for knowledge. Together we can create a culture of self improvement and a love of learning where if people want to get on, their first instinct is to improve their skills and education.

25. Our vision will be built on the following principles:

- investing in learning to benefit everyone;

- lifting barriers to learning;

- putting people first;

- sharing responsibility with employers, employees and the community;

- achieving world class standards and value for money; and

- working together as the key to success.

26. This consultation paper sets out how we propose to implement these principles in the Learning Age. We will:

- overcome barriers through new forms of delivering learning and better advice and information (Chapter One);

- support learners (Chapter Two);

- enable learning in the workplace (Chapter Three);

- involve further, higher and adult education and other partners in delivering our aims (Chapter Four);

- set high standards (Chapter Five);

- support learning through a better qualifications system (Chapter Six).

The way ahead

27. The creation of the Learning Age is a challenging and ambitious programme. It will require great effort but we have no doubt about the capacity or willingness of the nation to respond. We recognise that the uncertainty of change means that we cannot set out an unchanging blueprint in advance. One of the main areas for consultation concerns how the decisions and choices of individual learners and firms will require existing education and training institutions to transform themselves. The university, college or learning centre of the next century will look very different to that of the last. One of the aims of this paper, therefore, is to ask what shape these institutions will need to take in the years ahead in order to deliver our aims.

13

28. The Government has declared its commitment to the Learning Age. We will be judged on our success in creating a culture of self-improvement for the many and not the few. The main steps we are proposing are set out below. Further details on these and on the issues on which we are seeking views can be found in the main chapters.

29. Alongside this consultation paper - which sets out our vision - we will also be publishing a series of papers during the spring and summer on specific issues including:

Learning Age Papers

- *Higher Education for the 21st Century* (our response to the Dearing Report)
- *Further Education for the new Millennium* (our response to the Kennedy Report)
- Further education governance
- 16-19 planning
- University for Industry Pathfinder Prospectus
- The Careers Service
- 16-19 Qualifications
- Individual learning accounts development guide
- National Targets

Both *Higher Education for the 21st Century* and *Further Education for the new Millennium* are published alongside this Green Paper.

Consultation process

30. We are seeking views on any aspects of our proposals, and we would encourage everyone involved in learning to respond. In particular we would like your views on the questions set out in each Chapter and summarised in Chapter Seven, *Consultation: how to respond* (page 69). That Chapter also explains the different ways in which you can let us have your views. The deadline for comments is 24 July 1998.

Delivering our principles........

We propose to:

- **expand further and higher education** to provide for an extra 500,000 people by 2002;

- **make it easier for firms and individuals to learn by creating the University for Industry** and launch it in late 1999;

- **set up individual learning accounts** to encourage people to save to learn, and begin by allocating £150 million to support investment in learning accounts by one million people;

- **invest in young people** so that more continue to study beyond age 16;

- **double help for basic literacy and numeracy** skills amongst adults to involve over 500,000 adults a year by 2002;

- *widen participation in and access to learning* both in further, higher, adult, and community education (including residential provision), and through the UfI;

- *raise standards across teaching and learning* after the age of 16 through our new Training Standards Council, by ensuring implementation of the Dearing committee's standards proposals, and by inspection in further and adult education;

- *set and publish clear targets* for the skills and qualifications we want to achieve as a nation;

- *work with business, employees and their trade unions* to support and develop skills in the workplace;

- *build a qualifications system which is easily understood*, gives equal value to both academic and vocational learning, meets employers' and individuals' needs and promotes the highest standards.

The skills of the Learning Age.......

In the Learning Age we will need a workforce with imagination and confidence, and the skills required will be diverse: teachers and trainers to help us acquire these skills; carpenters and bricklayers to build the homes we need; designers and engineers who can create the products of the future, craftsmen and women to manufacture them, and people with the confidence to sell them right across the globe; researchers pushing at the frontiers of science and technology; scientists and technicians using the new technologies to help us communicate in ways unimaginable to our grandparents' generation; carers, nurses and doctors to heal and look after us; and musicians, artists, poets, writers and film-makers to lift our hearts and our horizons. All of these occupations - and thousands of others just as important - demand different types of knowledge and understanding and the skills to apply them. That is what we mean by skills, and it is through learning - with the help of those who teach us - that we acquire them.

"The country needs to develop a new learning culture, a culture of lifelong learning for all. It is essential to help ... all of its people meet the challenge they now face as they move towards the twenty-first century."

Professor Bob Fryer, National Advisory Group for Continuing Education and Lifelong Learning in *Learning for the Twenty-First Century* (DfEE, 1997).

1 The individual learning revolution

Putting learners first

1.1 The Fryer report called for a transformation of culture to achieve the Learning Age. The Government endorses that call and this consultation paper is the beginning of that process. Transforming our learning culture will depend on a partnership between individual responsibility and the wider community. As individuals and enterprises increasingly take charge of their own learning and of meeting their need for skills, they will require support to enable them to achieve their goals, including better access.

1.2 In future, learners need not be tied to particular locations. They will be able to study at home, at work, or in a local library or shopping centre, as well as in colleges and universities. People will be able to study at a distance using broadcast media and on-line access. Our aim should be to help people to learn wherever they choose and support them in assessing how they are doing and where they want to go next.

1.3 Demand is potentially vast. When asked, companies and individuals say they want to improve their skills. And many do. People learn for a variety of reasons; it could be to change career, to increase earning power, to update skills, or simply for the joy of learning itself. Last year about eight million adults studied in colleges, universities, on training courses delivered through Training and Enterprise Councils (TECs) or at evening classes. This is a good start, but we must do better. Many more people could be involved in learning but are not because they face barriers. We are seeking views on how these can be overcome.

Overcoming the obstacles

1.4 We need to understand better the obstacles people face. Among those most commonly cited are time, cost, fear, inadequate information, complexity, and inconvenience. For smaller businesses in particular, the costs and complexity of providing learning for their employees can be daunting. Individual learners are also deterred by a sense that learning is 'not for them', and yet the benefits of learning are significant.

1.5 One of our biggest challenges is to get all those who provide learning to make it easier for people to learn. This can be done by:

- encouraging people to have *higher expectations* of themselves and of others;

- providing learning at a *time and a place to suit* the individual or firm (for example, seven days a week all year round, as the Open University does);

- ensuring that all learning has *high standards of teaching and training*;

- providing *information and advice* to people to clear a way through the jungle of jargon and initials;

- *making learning welcoming*;

- *giving people the support they need* in order to learn; for instance by helping with the cost of childcare, or the cost of learning, or with access for someone who has a disability;

- *providing qualifications for adults that are easily understood*, meet employers' and individuals' needs, encourage learning, and are flexible so that individuals can obtain qualifications in stages; and

- recognising that, over time, *institutions and ways of doing things will need to change* in response to the needs of learners.

Q. Are there other obstacles that people face?

Q. Do the steps outlined above cover the main changes that are needed to make learning easier?

The University for Industry

1.6 The capacity to cope with change will be the hallmark of success in the twenty-first century. In the global marketplace the UK cannot compete on the basis of low wages and low added value. Rather, we will need to provide better quality goods and services, high added value and productivity, and be able to use technology to the full. This will require investment in the skills and abilities of management and workforce alike; and also the creation of new enthusiasm for learning. It is to help do this that we are establishing an entirely new type of institution - the University for Industry - which will put the UK ahead of the rest of the world in using new technology to improve learning and skills.

1.7 The UfI will connect those who want to learn with ways of doing so. It will act as the hub of a brand new learning network, using modern communication technologies to link businesses and individuals to cost-effective, accessible and flexible education and training.

1.8 People and companies will be able to contact the University for Industry by telephone, letter, fax, email (through the UfI's website) or by calling at a UfI enquiry desk in, for example, a supermarket, high street shop, college, TEC or Business Link. The UfI will tell you what learning is available and offer advice if you need it, and provide you with a course that meets your needs, whether full-time, part-time, or through study at home, at work or at a local learning centre. For example, it could deliver a learning package on a CD-ROM to your home or send it by email, or contract with a college for an evening class, or broadcast an interactive TV programme, or provide a course over the radio or on the Internet. Students will not need to be tied to one particular location.

1.9 With 99 per cent of households having a television set, broadcasting has enormous potential to open up access to learning through the Ufl; for example, the BBC's *Computers Don't Bite* campaign to encourage people to use computers reached seven million people, with 150,000 people calling the helpline for guidance. The Discovery Channel, and the History and National Geographic Channels illustrate the demand and potential for specialist channels and programming which informs. By harnessing broadcasting to enable people to learn at home, the Ufl will help to overcome people's fears about learning.

1.10 The Ufl learner will also be able to study through learning centres. These will be places equipped with technology where people can go and access Ufl courses and materials. The centres should be within easy reach of most people's homes. They could be in their firm, in a library, shopping centre, or football club, or at a school or further education college (we are investing £5 million to develop learning centres in colleges in 1998-99). The Ufl will ensure that learning centres meet the high standard required for providing access to Ufl programmes. Like any other learning institution, the Ufl will look after its learners, offering advice and support to businesses

and individuals. Everyone who takes a course through the Ufl will become a Ufl 'student'.

1.11 Stimulating mass demand will be a major task for the Ufl. There will be an extensive advertising and marketing campaign to attract individual and business customers to this initiative. During its early years, the Ufl will focus on priority target areas identified by industry, learning providers and the Government. These are likely to cover:

- basic skills;

- information technology skills;

- the management of small and medium-sized businesses; and

- skill needs in specific industries and services.

1.12 The Ufl will also explore with learners and suppliers gaps in provision and then commission courses to fill them. These courses will be supplied to the Ufl by further education colleges, private learning providers, universities and colleges of higher education, education publishers, broadcasters and others.

1.13 The Government will provide funding to support the Ufl in a private-public partnership and will help meet the learning costs of people on low incomes. Individual learning accounts (see Chapter Two) will be available to help people to save to pay for courses. TECs may assist some businesses in using the Ufl. Everyone who takes out an individual learning account will automatically receive information about the Ufl.

1.14 The Ufl will make a unique contribution to the learning revolution. Just as the Open University helped transform attitudes to higher education in the 1970s, so the University for Industry will help change attitudes to learning and acquiring skills in the new century. The Ufl will directly address the obstacles identified earlier. It will:

- *overcome complexity* by offering a one-stop shop for advice about what is available and courses that meet learners' needs;

- *reduce fear* by enabling people to learn at home, one-to-one;

- *save time* by delivering learning in a way and at a pace that suits the learner; and

- *reduce costs* by creating a mass market for learning products, sharing resources across industrial sectors and particular skills.

1.15 A Ufl Transition Team will shortly be established, made up of experts in skills, marketing and finance, and more details will be published in the spring in the Ufl Pathfinder Prospectus. This will set out how people interested in supporting the Ufl's establishment can get involved.

Q. **How can we raise awareness of what the Ufl has to offer individual learners and businesses?**

Q. **Which people and businesses should the Ufl target in particular?**

Q. **How can we best link the Ufl with individual learning accounts?**

Q. **Should the Ufl focus exclusively on using new technology to deliver learning?**

Piloting the UfI approach......

The *Sunderland University for Industry Project* is now piloting the UfI idea in an exciting new project. It has developed from the Institute for Public Policy Research (IPPR) report, *The University for Industry: creating an National Learning Network* (IPPR, 1996).

The pilot project puts learning right at the centre of people's lives - using commercial marketing techniques to sell learning and to link people into new and existing educational opportunities. Information, advice and registration are available via a free telephone helpline operating seven days a week. The 'one-stop shop' approach provides flexible access to hundreds of courses, materials and free tasters, such as *IT for the Terrified* and *Time Management*.

People can learn on their own when it suits them, on-line over the Internet, or meet a tutor. Learning takes place at work or at 35 learning centres in colleges, schools and libraries, as well as shopping centres and the local football stadium.

A sophisticated computer 'virtual engine' supports the call centre with a courses database and immediate enquiry and registration facilities. Using the Internet a range of instant statistics are provided such as learners' details, course bookings and progression routes. There have been over 1,400 registrations in the first four months. The project has created a network of local, regional and national stakeholders, including companies, voluntary agencies, the BBC, the NHS, Sunderland City Council and Sunderland City TEC. The project is funded via a public-private partnership.

The *Bradford Virtual College* - a partnership between the local authority, companies (particularly in the technology field), the TEC, local schools, colleges and the university - is already helping to make it easier for people at work to learn and update their skills. In three years it has developed multi-media training packages in partnership with local industry and awarding bodies. Learners undertaking NVQs through the Virtual College can get their work assessed on-line and soon they will be able to book places on practical workshops at local further education colleges without leaving their workplace. They can also get comprehensive on-line and telephone support from practising trainers or help with technical difficulties, such as hardware, software, installation or networking problems.

So far over 250 employed people and 65 unemployed people have gained NVQs; 55 people who were unemployed have got jobs. Training needs and barriers to progress have been identified and innovative solutions - hardware and software - developed locally. One of the partner companies - Chase Advanced Technologies - has introduced financial incentives for employees who gain NVQs through the system. Productivity has improved since they became involved, with higher output month on month, no increase in costs and no drop in quality.

Learning Direct

1.16 As a first step towards the Ufl, we are taking action to overcome one of the main barriers to learning - getting easy access to information about what is available. Learning Direct - a new national telephone helpline - offers advice both on how to get started and on courses to suit individual needs.

> ### Learning Direct
> *call freephone 0800 100 900*
> *9am-9pm Monday to Friday and*
> *9am-12 noon Saturday*

1.17 Learning Direct is:

- free all over the UK. 0800 100 900 serves England, Wales, Scotland and Northern Ireland;

- up-to-date, high quality and accurate;

- confidential - it will not pass on call details;

- impartial - it is there to help the caller, not to push a product or promote a particular institution or to sell anything; and

- staffed by experienced advisors.

1.18 Learning Direct is for everyone - for people in work or out of work, professionals, skilled, unskilled, male, female - in fact for anyone over 18 years old. It is particularly designed to help people who find it difficult to access learning, or just do not know how. There are special arrangements for people with additional needs: for example, a minicom for people with a hearing impairment and a Braille facility for people who are visually impaired.

1.19 Learning Direct can refer people to local advice services, adult education, further and higher education, and private providers. It also links up with careers guidance at local level, and with the advice offered to individuals by TECs, local education authorities (LEAs), the Youth Service and the Employment Service.

1.20 Employers can benefit too. Learning Direct can advise them and give them information about qualifications, training or development for their employees. Learning Direct can also offer some help to organisations which advise others, for example, libraries and Citizens' Advice Bureaux.

1.21 Learning Direct will become the Ufl information and advice service when the Ufl opens for business.

Q. How can Learning Direct best fit in with local sources of advice?

Technology and learning

1.22 As the Ufl will demonstrate, one of the best ways to overcome some of the barriers to learning will be to use new broadcasting and other technologies. We expect their role in learning more generally to increase significantly.

1.23 We currently lead Europe, and possibly the world, in learning technology and flexible learning delivery, and we intend to help maintain that lead. Through the British Educational Communications and

Technology Agency (BECTA), we are encouraging learning providers to use information technology and evaluate it. We are also supporting a new quality system for providers of flexible learning being developed by the British Association for Open Learning.

1.24 New digital technology will allow many more channels to be received, whether by satellite, cable or terrestrial TV, and will open the way to interactive learning. Broadcasters have large archives of educational programming which, once digitised, could be made widely available. Linking digital pictures with support materials and remote tuition, for example over the Internet, is already possible. We are opening up discussions with broadcasters, the cable industry and others about ways in which their programme-making capacity and digital networks could support interactive learning. The BBC has already announced plans to launch a public service educational channel - BBC Learning - which will be freely available alongside other digital programming.

1.25 Interactive learning 'products' will have considerable export potential, building on the existing success of television programme sales. We also have a proven ability to recruit students from abroad into further and higher education. There will be opportunities to accredit overseas courses, a growing demand for English language teaching, and the prospect of providing tuition, courses, lectures, and learning materials for sale across the world with the support of the British Council. There is great potential for the United Kingdom to become a world beater in this new global industry.

1.26 We are also setting up the National Grid for Learning. This will help teachers and students in schools to gain access to a wide range of learning materials on-line. The Grid will include the Virtual Teachers' Centre - a resource on the Internet to help improve school teacher training and curriculum support. As well as being available directly to schools, the Grid will also provide links to the UfI. There will also be access from the Grid to JANET and SuperJANET, the wide-band network used by universities.

Q. How can Government and broadcasters maximise the contribution broadcasting can make to widening access to learning?

Q. In what other ways can broadcasting and new information technologies support the Learning Age?

Priorities for early action:

We propose to:

- launch the University for Industry;

- stimulate increased demand for learning through the new University for Industry;

- publicise the Learning Direct information, advice and guidance service; and

- work with broadcasters to promote learning channels.

The Learning Age will require new ways of supporting learners. Investing in learning benefits everyone so it should be a shared responsibility. We will encourage employers and individuals to take greater responsibility and will target public funds for student support on learners in greatest need.

2 Investing in Learning

Principles for public funding

2.1 After nearly two decades of inadequate investment in learning, we face a major challenge. The Government has already shown its commitment to education as its priority by announcing an additional £165 million for higher education and £100 million for further education in 1998-99, and by its pledge to support an extra 500,000 people in further and higher education by 2002. We are seeking views on a new partnership between Government, individuals and employers for further investment in the future.

2.2 Individuals, employers and the state should all contribute, directly or through earnings foregone, to the cost of learning over a lifetime because all gain from this investment. Individuals enhance their employability and skills, businesses improve their productivity, and society enjoys wider social and economic benefits.

2.3 The aim of public funding should be to widen participation and increase attainment at all levels where this will benefit society most; for example, investment in the highest levels of postgraduate research strengthens our competitiveness. We propose the following priorities for public funding:

- we will guarantee help with basic skills, with courses provided free at whatever age;

- we will guarantee free full-time education for young people up to the age of 18;

- we will share with employers the cost of learning for young people in work (for example, Modern Apprenticeships);

- we will share the cost of higher education with students through our new student support system;

- we will make provision for the highest level of postgraduate education; and

- we will target financial help for adults on those who need it most.

2.4 Public financial support for learners should be designed to: bring back into learning those who stopped after leaving school; address particular shortages; widen access for those who are disadvantaged; and enable individuals to choose the method of learning that suits them best. For other adults, the main responsibility will rest with them and their employers. The Government's role will be to provide incentives to adults to undertake training through individual learning accounts.

2.5 Individuals should invest in their own learning to improve their employability, professional competence, and earning potential or for leisure. Employers will continue to have responsibility for investing in the job and career-related training of their employees, although some public funding of employee training may be justified to promote broader learning and portable qualifications where this benefits the economy.

2.6 We will allocate public funding so as to encourage providers to find new, flexible and cost-effective methods of responding to individuals' learning needs. We will reward them for retaining people in learning, for raising achievement and for excellence; and we will seek maximum leverage from others. We will also aim for greater consistency so that different providers get a similar balance of funding from the public purse, individuals and employers.

2.7 We expect all providers to continue to improve their efficiency in delivering learning. Co-operation between learning providers, between employer and employee, and between Government and the private sector will be the key to creative and effective use of funds from all sources.

2.8 We intend to make better use of the substantial sums which are currently invested nationally and locally, and of the resources in our schools, colleges and universities. Much more could be done to open up facilities outside normal teaching hours and term time (for example, evenings and weekends) and to use school premises, provided that this does not compromise the security of the schools' pupils and staff. In Chapter Four we propose that partners in every area should work together to agree local access plans; these could also cover other community-based resources.

Q. Are our funding principles the right ones?

Q. Are there further steps we should be taking to improve the balance of investment in learning between employers, individuals and the public purse?

Q. Is it realistic to expect individuals or employers to invest more? If so, what form should this additional investment take?

Sharing investment with individuals

2.9 Many people who take up learning - whether a training course or a university degree - already pay fees or meet other costs. People at work increasingly invest in their own career development. Our radical proposals for a national system of individual learning accounts will lead the way for people to take control of this investment in their own future. They will also make providers more responsive to learners' needs.

Individual learning accounts

2.10 Learning accounts will be built on two key principles: first, that individuals are best placed to choose what and how they want to learn; and second, that responsibility for investing in learning is shared.

2.11 A national system of individual learning accounts will turn these principles into reality, acting as a catalyst for the learning revolution. They will allow individuals to save and borrow for investment in their own learning. Learning accounts will be available to everyone, including the self-employed. They will be used, at the learner's choice, to pay for learning - whether an evening class, or a learning programme bought through the Ufl, or meeting the cost of childcare so as to give time to study.

2.12 The Government will construct the framework for these accounts so as to encourage as many people as possible to save using them. In the medium term, this could be done through tax incentives or by matching the individual's contributions with public support. We will be consulting widely with the financial services sector to achieve this. Having created the framework, we expect that learning accounts will be offered through a range of financial institutions. We are currently working with these institutions on development plans. It is important that people should have a choice about where they want to hold their account.

2.13 We will also explore the best way of helping people to make informed decisions about their learning using their learning account. The Ufl will play an important role. For the first time, individuals and companies will have one place to get advice on the courses they need, what their account could buy them and which providers are right for them. We will explore how the University for Industry and learning accounts can best dovetail, and

---

ILAs in action....

Denise McManus is a Senior Customer Adviser for Liverpool Victoria Friendly Society, an insurance company based in Bournemouth. She supports new staff in the firm's call centre after their initial training period. Aiming to encourage its employees back into learning, the company is pioneering individual learning accounts, with the help of Dorset TEC. Staff are offered a career development interview with the Careers Service and £200 to go into their own learning account for agreed learning as long as they invest £25 themselves. As an incentive, staff get an extra £50 bonus on completion of their studies.

For a while, Denise was seconded to the company's training department where she designed and delivered training. She enjoyed this work so much that she has now decided to use her learning account to pursue a Certificate in Training Proficiency. She would like a professional qualification to further a career in training.

Thirty people at one site enquired about registering for learning accounts within three days of Liverpool Victoria's offer being made.

how smart card technology can help people to manage their financial transactions and to plan and record their learning in relation both to their learning account and their 'membership' of the Ufl.

2.14 We will test different approaches to learning accounts in preparing for a national system. For this work to provide useful answers, we need to test real reactions to different forms of learning accounts. As part of this work, and to provide impetus to learning accounts, we propose to support up to one million learning accounts, funded by £150 million from TECs' resources. These will be based on two main approaches to learning accounts: the *universal* and the *targeted.*

- the *universal* approach will offer accounts to anyone at work wanting to learn. Everyone will have to invest a minimum amount of their own money in their account, either as a lump sum or in the form of a commitment to regular saving. The Government will then support that initial investment, up to a maximum public contribution of £150 for each account. It will be open to others - for example, employers - to contribute to a person's account in cash or in kind;

- the *targeted* approach will use a proportion of these one million accounts to support particular learning or skill needs; for example, people without qualifications and in low-skill jobs, areas of skills shortage, employees in small firms, and those seeking to return to work.

2.15 We also want to encourage more people to study at sub-degree level as Graduate Apprentices and, in particular, people in employment who might not otherwise have taken up higher education. We intend to pilot, in a few sectors, approaches that - using learning accounts to provide incentive and support - will encourage people to study while they are employed.

2.16 Learning accounts have the potential to play a very significant role in developing a new partnership between public funding for learning and the investment made by individuals and employers. It may be sensible to channel some of the funding which currently goes to providers - for example, TECs or further education colleges - through learning accounts. This might increase both choice for individuals and total funding by providing a greater incentive to individuals and businesses to match the Government's investment. We propose to discuss with the relevant partners possible projects to explore this.

2.17 Individual learning accounts could have a profound effect on the way individuals take responsibility for their learning and on the incentive for institutions to respond to individuals' needs. To do so, learning accounts will need to be part of a coherent approach to welfare reform, in which relieving poverty is not just a question of financial support but also of enabling people to get the skills which allow them to earn their own living. They therefore raise some fundamental questions:

- how effective would fiscal incentives be in encouraging greater investment in learning?

- should these incentives be targeted or universally available?

- what public funds should be channelled through learning accounts?

- how should learning accounts relate to other incentives to save, including individual savings accounts (ISAs)?

- what incentives should there be for employers to contribute to learning accounts, given the existing tax relief on their expenditure on training employees?

- how can we ensure that individuals have the information they need to use their learning accounts effectively?

2.18 Working with our partners, and especially TECs and the financial services sector, we will pilot a range of different approaches across the country to ensure that the learning account framework we develop is flexible and cost effective.

Q. **How should learning accounts and the learning smart card be developed to help people invest in and manage their own learning?**

Q. **On what basis should the Government's contribution to up to one million accounts be allocated?**

Q. **What will be needed to make learning accounts attractive to people, both financially and through the other advantages they will bring?**

Q. **Should learning accounts be used in future to channel other forms of public support for learners?**

Support for students

2.19 The principle that the costs of learning should be shared applies equally to students and their families. The student support system has, in the past, distributed public help unevenly. People should not be prevented from taking up learning because of personal or family financial hardship, but they also benefit from learning in the form of higher earning potential.

2.20 We are examining ways of providing greater incentives to stay in learning - by better targeting of support - for young people and their families in low income households. This will include those who have just left compulsory education. In further education, learning will remain free for young people up to the age of 18, and for adults who are unemployed, on income support or dependent on those who are. We will look for increasing contributions from employers for courses directly meeting their skill needs.

2.21 In July 1997 we announced new financial support arrangements for full-time undergraduate students. Students will in future be expected to contribute up to £1,000 per year towards the cost of their tuition, depending on their own, their parents' or their spouse's income. Students from poorer families will have their fees paid for them, and an additional loan of at least £1,000 for maintenance will be available to students and their families so that no parental contribution need be greater than it is at the moment. The new arrangements are fairer and will help to ensure that all students have access to financial support when they need it most. No-one will be prevented from entering higher education because of their financial circumstances.

2.22 Student loans are currently not available to people who are over the age of 50 at the start of their course. We do not think it would be appropriate to make income-contingent loans available to students who do not plan to re-enter the labour market following their studies and so would not be in a position to repay. However, we are minded to extend loans to people in their early 50s wishing to undertake a course of higher education; for example, to help them retrain following redundancy. We would welcome views on the priority which should be given to such an extension.

2.23 Graduates will not start to repay their loans until their income is £10,000 a year, and repayment, through the Inland Revenue, will be entirely linked to income. For many graduates this will mean smaller monthly repayments over a longer period than under the current loans scheme. In the few cases where loans have not been paid off by the age of 65, they will be cancelled so long as the borrower is not in default. We propose to make the administration of student support more efficient so that students receive their loans by the start of term.

2.24 Financial support can also make the difference for many people seeking to return to learning in further and higher education. Access funds help students in financial difficulties to meet the costs of accommodation, childcare, transport, books and equipment, or other costs. We propose to increase the size of access funds in further education and to consider whether to distribute them differently. In higher education, we have already announced a £36 million access package which will benefit part-time students and those facing particular hardship. This will allow us to:

- double the amount in access funds for students facing hardship and extend eligibility to part-timers;

- abolish the means test currently applied to special grants for disabled full-time students;

- introduce an additional £250 loan on a discretionary basis for students who find themselves in financial difficulties; and

- pay the fees of part-time students who lose their job after starting their course.

2.25 In adult, further and higher education we propose to change the current system for discretionary awards provided by local education authorities. It is inequitable that the chances of getting an award depend on where you live. We have asked a group of local authority, further education, and other representatives to advise on a more effective way of targeting the resources available on those students most in need. In addition to these new arrangements - on which we will consult - local education authorities will continue to be able to make their own discretionary awards if they wish.

2.26 Career Development Loans (CDLs) help people to pay for vocational education or training by offering a deferred repayment bank loan. They are available through a partnership between the Government and four major banks. From this April we will change the terms to enable a longer interest holiday - for people who are unemployed, or working but in receipt of in-work benefits - after their period of learning. In due course, we will consult the banks on Career Development Loans becoming part of the individual learning account system.

Q. **What would be the most effective way of targeting financial support so that more young people from low-income families stay on in full-time education after 16?**

Q. **Should support loans be made available to undergraduate students in their early 50s?**

Q. **Are the steps we are taking sufficient to create a fair and effective system of student support?**

Sharing investment with employers

2.27 The costs and benefits of investment in skills should be shared between the Government and employers. This is already reflected in contributions to young people's learning in the workplace. In Modern Apprenticeships employers invest in their future workforce skills with support from TECs. The same principle will apply to National Traineeships, and in the New Deal for the under-25s where employers will meet some of the learning and other costs for young people in subsidised jobs. From next September, for employee training which directly benefits individual employers, further education colleges will share this cost equally with employers by increasing fees. This will bring in an estimated additional £20 million next year, rising after that. Colleges will invest this income to help increase access.

2.28 Employers will also have an opportunity to support their employees in learning by contributing to their individual learning accounts. We will strongly encourage employers to do so, and to offer other support, such as time off, in order to assist their employees to learn.

Childcare

2.29 Many adults face extra costs associated with learning. The most significant cost for many of them - particularly women - wishing to return to the labour market and improve their skills is paying for childcare. We want to support parents in taking up education, training or work by ensuring that a range of good quality affordable provision is available in every neighbourhood. This is a major challenge.

2.30 We will publish in the first half of this year our proposals for a national childcare strategy, inviting views on its implementation. This will include consideration of how some of the £300 million package over five years announced in the Chancellor's Pre-Budget Report can be used to offer quality childcare to support those in learning. Individual learning accounts will also be available to help pay for the cost of childcare.

Priorities for early action

We propose to:

- judge priorities for public spending against our principles for shared investment in learning;

- provide funds for an additional 500,000 people in further and higher education;

- introduce individual learning accounts - linked to learning smart cards - to help people take responsibility for investing in their own learning;

- offer one million learning accounts a starter contribution of up to £150 each;

- implement our new arrangements for student support in higher education;

- help young people and adults in financial hardship to meet costs associated with learning, including through a new system for discretionary awards; and

- consult on our childcare strategy.

In the Learning Age individuals and their employers will share a responsibility for increasing the quality and quantity of learning at work. We will support employers, employees, and self-employed people in meeting this challenge.

3 Learning at Work

Skills for the knowledge-based economy

3.1 In the Learning Age, equipping people with the right knowledge and skills will be crucial to maintaining high and sustainable levels of employment and price stability. It will also improve productivity. This Chapter looks at how learning in the workplace needs to be transformed to achieve this.

3.2 Many leading employers educate and train their workforce to the standards of their best competitors. Others - especially in smaller firms - carry out little training. In 1993 the total investment in training by employers of ten or more people was £10.6 billion. The vast majority of employers provide some training to their workforce, but this investment is unevenly spread and variable in quality. Younger employees and those who already have good educational qualifications receive more training. People with degrees are over six times more likely to be trained than people with no qualifications. For people working in very small firms, the prospect of their receiving training is substantially less.

The national framework

3.3 Transforming learning in the workplace will primarily be for employers, employees and the self-employed to achieve. The Government will help people to invest in learning by lifting barriers to access and improving the quality of support available to businesses and individuals. We will combine effective pressure and support within an effective legislative framework. We have recently announced plans to strengthen this framework by legislating to ensure that all 16 and 17 year-old employees can undertake education and training up to NVQ level 2 (if they are not already there) - see Chapter Four.

3.4 We will maintain the statutory powers of the Construction Industry Training Board and the Engineering Construction Industry Training Board to raise a levy from employers to fund training. We note an encouraging trend in other sectors for this to happen on a voluntary basis; for example, SKILLSET runs a levy in the broadcasting and film industry to ensure that there are enough trained freelance technicians. We will support those industries that wish to strengthen training in this way.

Setting targets

3.5 Targets provide a focus for action and a benchmark for progress. We believe they will help employers and employees in changing the culture in many workplaces. We propose to set new targets in three areas:

- *young people:* just over 70 per cent of 19 year-olds reach a level 2 qualification and 48 per cent of 21 year olds reach level 3. Significant further progress is needed to match world-class standards;

- *adults:* 42 per cent of the workforce have a level 3 qualification and 24 per cent have level 4. This is well short of the current targets (60 per cent at level 3 and 30 per cent at level 4) and of what is needed for a competitive economy; and

- *employers:* the present target focuses on reaching the Investors in People National Standard as the main measure of employers' development of the people who work for them. 76 per cent of organisations employing more than 200 employees and 40 per cent of those employing 50 or more have either reached the National Standard or are committed to it.

3.6 We are currently consulting on options for new national targets and would welcome comments on what these targets should be. (For a copy of the consultative document *Targets for our future*, call 0845 60 222 60.) Once the new targets are agreed, we will work closely with industry, with the support of the National Advisory Council for Education and Training Targets, to meet them.

3.7 We intend to monitor progress regularly to see what further steps might be required to ensure that the needs of the economy are met. We must ensure that sustainable economic growth is not constrained by a lack of skills, and that the level of education and training in the workplace matches that of the best among our competitors.

Supporting learning businesses

3.8 Learning assists organisations in three ways. It raises skill levels and, through the process of learning itself, can help organisations respond to change; the successful firm of the future will know 'how' to learn as much as 'what' to learn. It also increases the knowledge base of the organisation, which is essential to discovery and innovation.

3.9 Some organisations have already turned their workplaces into centres of learning by providing employees with skills beyond those needed for immediate business objectives. Employee development schemes - pioneered by management and trade unions in Ford, Rover, and Sheffield City Council among others and now being taken up elsewhere - have been very successful in encouraging employees to learn. Firms such as Anglian Water, Motorola Ltd and British Aerospace have set up company learning centres - places where employees can study, with access to support, materials and advice. The Fryer report recommends the widespread establishment of company learning centres with strong links to the University for Industry. We propose to encourage this in both the public and private sectors, supported by individual learning accounts. Investors in People UK is launching a review of how best to incorporate approaches like this into the National Standard.

3.10 Learning is a natural issue for partnership in the workplace between employers, employees and their trade unions. Businesses, with their desire for improved competitiveness, and employees, concerned with job security and future prospects, have a shared interest in learning. This joint activity, focusing on practical issues such as time off for learning, employer support for individual learning accounts, and training plans for staff, signals a new and modern role for unions.

3.11 Trade unions have long made a valuable contribution to workplace education. Through this route many employees are encouraged to become interested in learning, leading on, for example, to further study in higher education or at residential colleges. We propose to support innovative projects in workplace education by establishing an Employee Education Development Fund. We will allocate £2 million to this fund next year and will discuss with the Trades Union Congress (TUC) how it can most effectively be used. This could include unions contracting with the University for Industry to deliver training.

3.12 The Learning Age will not just be about the 'top' of organisations spreading the message. It will be as much about encouraging demand for learning from the bottom up. For example, the TUC's Bargaining for Skills initiative, which now involves projects with about 60 TECs, is leading the way in helping trade union representatives negotiate with employers about improving training.

Q. How should we develop the national framework for learning at work? Are the measures we propose sufficient to meet the challenge?

Q. What role could incentives play in encouraging investment by employers in workplace learning?

Q. What contribution can businesses make to wider learning?

Q. How can we encourage employers to offer more of their employees the chance to gain qualifications at work?

Q. What measures are needed to ensure that people in work have the time they need to learn?

Q. How can employers be encouraged to contribute to their employees' individual learning accounts?

Workplace partnership in action.....

As a result of the *TUC's Bargaining for Skills* programme, supported by CEWTEC (the TEC for East Cheshire and the Wirral), the food company Horizon Biscuits agreed with the Transport and General Workers' Union (TGWU) to introduce a food processing NVQ and set up a learning centre on site. Already nearly one third of staff have enrolled on time study learning programmes and 100 candidates have volunteered for NVQs.

"It has been a real success story for both the union and the company. We have been helped enormously by TUC Bargaining for Skills which not only helped us identify what we wanted, but also brought us together with the college and the TEC, without whom the learning centre would not have been possible." Richie James - TGWU Convenor

"The Bargaining for Skills programme has been a vital first step in the conversion of the company's culture so that we recognise the need for personal skills development programmes to be linked to the company's business development plan." Don Helsby - Manufacturing Services Manager.

Another example is *UNISON's Return to Learn programme* which has been running since 1989. It offers educational opportunities to union members who missed out in the education system. Return to Learn is provided through the union's Open College which adopts a 'passport' approach to learning, giving all members access to flexible learning at the appropriate level. The union has also developed a Return to Learn Partnership where employers commit themselves to working with the union to improve education and training. By 1996 around 3,000 students had completed Return to Learn courses.

The Return to Learn programme also provides a stepping stone into higher education. Students gain admission to university either through an accumulation of Return to Learn credits or via a one year union access course. As part of this programme UNISON has developed special links with the University of Warwick and the University of East London.

Helping small firms to learn

3.13 The best small firms in Britain lead their European equivalents in training and development, but there is a long tail of small businesses which do little or no training at all. A recent study[1] of small and medium size firms found that 20 per cent of the firms surveyed in the UK saw no need to raise their level of training compared with just four per cent in France and six per cent in Germany.

3.14 There are a number of reasons for this. Small firms say they cannot readily find cover to release people for learning off-the-job in working hours. They lack the time and expertise to organise the right opportunities. Individually they cannot influence private or further education sector providers to offer the right education and training. They do not have the purchasing power to keep down the costs of training. Too often training and development take second place to short-term survival, and yet the business benefits to small firms are tangible.

3.15 We want to help change the culture in small firms by linking learning more closely with business performance and by lifting obstacles to learning. This will be a major role for the University for Industry. The UfI will be able to deliver custom-made learning to the enterprise, and employees will be able to use individual learning accounts to support their own career development. As one way of making Investors in People more accessible to small firms, Investors in People UK is working with selected firms to demonstrate the business benefits of involving their suppliers in the Standard. TECs will focus on small and medium size businesses in their workforce development plans and encourage the take up of Modern Apprenticeships and National Traineeships.

Q. What more should be done to improve learning in small firms and organisations?

Q. What steps could be taken to provide cover for small firms to allow employees to undertake training?

Small firms and the learning habit.....

J and K Ross is a small family firm in Warrington supplying safety equipment. It introduced a new training programme - involving workshops, individual tutorials, indoor and outdoor group exercises, and personal training logs - after a company health check showed they needed to invest in their employees' skills. Profits rose by 40 per cent and turnover by 20 per cent while customer complaints fell by 24 per cent. The company won a National Training Award.

Sales director, Chris Ross, said: "We have always been an organisation that prided itself on offering the best possible service within a family business ethos. But we also wanted to grow and still maintain our original standards. The training approach we have adopted has allowed us to achieve just that."

---

[1] Review of training and management development in SMEs in the UK and Europe (TEC National Council/Grant Thornton, 1997).

Investors in People

3.16 Investors in People is the most widely recognised tool for organisations to plan for the current and future development of their staff to meet business aims. It also has a clear link with improved business performance. At the end of December 1997 there were 8,600 organisations recognised as Investors in People with a further 21,500 formally committed to the National Standard. Together they cover around 30 per cent of people employed in Britain.

3.18 We will look at the best way of strengthening the links between adoption of Investors in People and Government business support. Good human resource practice among our contractors should improve their ability to meet our needs; we wish to encourage that. Our aim is that every Government Department should be an Investor in People by the year 2000.

Q. Are there any other steps that we could take to increase the take-up of Investors in People?

Investors in People and improved business performance......

Auto Flow Services Ltd - which provides warehousing and stock management for the automotive industry - is an Investor in People and a 1997 National Training Award winner. By investing in its workforce it has increased turnover by 37 per cent, doubled its profits and reduced customer complaints to 0.06 per cent. It now employs over 80 staff.

Brian Seal, Quality and Training Manager, says "We now have a multi-skilled workforce willing and keen to develop further."

3.17 We propose to consolidate the position of Investors in People as the general standard across the public and private sectors, and in large and small organisations. In particular we would like to see all our leading companies recognised as Investors in People, as well as using other tools for improving performance such as the Business Excellence model (the British version of the European Framework for Quality Management). Almost all of the top 50 UK companies have some part of their organisation committed to, or recognised as, Investors in People, but progress in many of these companies is far from complete. This is one priority for action by Investors in People UK, alongside improving access for small employers.

Better information

3.19 One way to help raise standards is to collect information about current performance, and this is why we propose that companies should publish better information about their investment in skills. Business, employees, and investors all have an interest in this. The Government needs to know how the nation as a whole is performing, given the importance of skills for our economic future.

3.20 We are working with the Confederation of British Industry (CBI) and others to develop a system for benchmarking information on training investment. We want organisations' annual reports to reflect their level of investment in human capital. We propose to discuss with Investors in People UK, the Auditing Standards Board and business how they might support greater transparency of information about training.

Q. What measurements should be used to best assess investment in training?

Q. How should this information be publicised?

Developing skills

3.21 The Learning Age will be built on a wide range of skills, knowledge and understanding, from the most basic skills of literacy and numeracy right up to graduate and postgraduate level. As well as the demand for highly specialised and technical jobs at the frontiers of knowledge, there will also continue to be a large number of jobs providing service and support on which society depends. Business success will increasingly depend on people having the right skills in the right place at the right time. In order to ensure that we have the skills necessary for sustainable economic growth, we propose to take the following steps.

National Skills Task Force

3.22 We are setting up a National Skills Task Force, working with a new Skills Unit in the Department for Education and Employment. The Task Force will:

- assess future skill needs so that the economy has the skills it requires;

- strengthen partnership at regional and local level, share information and co-ordinate action to improve the supply of skills;

- ensure that accurate information on changing skill needs is effectively disseminated; and

- work with the new National Training Organisations (NTOs), the University for Industry and others to tackle skill shortages.

Q. Which priority skill areas should the National Skills Task Force focus on initially?

Basic skills

3.23 Few people in the United Kingdom cannot read, write or handle numbers at all, but around one in five of all adults has poor literacy and numeracy skills. People with poor basic skills are at a disadvantage in coping with the complex demands of modern life. They are more likely to be unemployed, to receive social security benefits, and to have low incomes, and less likely to get promotion or a new job. Our target is that by 2002 we will be helping over 500,000 people a year (more than twice the current number) to improve their basic skills.

3.24 We propose to expand the help already given through further and adult education (where all specific basic skills courses are free). Many students on vocational courses need additional help with literacy and numeracy. The Investing in Young People programme and the New Deal for unemployed young people aged 18 to 24, together with our continuing provision for older adults who are unemployed and lack skills, will all focus on basic skills.

3.25 Returning to learn, particularly basic skills, can be daunting. Different people respond to different ways of teaching.

We will therefore pilot a range of new approaches by investing over £4 million a year in the Basic Skills Agency to support innovation, and £5 million in basic skills summer schools for 1998. The Agency is currently piloting new ways of helping families to improve numeracy, and we will use our family literacy programmes to help parents improve their skills while they help their children. The Standards Fund will provide resources to expand these schemes to reach some 6,000 parents and their children in 125 LEAs in 1998-99. We are inviting Sir Claus Moser, Chairman of the Basic Skills Agency, to chair a working group to advise on effective post-school basic skills provision. He will consult with the Literacy and Numeracy Strategy Group to ensure a complementary approach to that in schools. The University for Industry will support all of this work by giving early priority to helping people already in the workforce who have literacy and numeracy difficulties.

3.26 For many adult offenders learning provides a second chance. Education and training will form a fuller part of the new constructive regimes in prison, to which the Government attaches great importance. They will also be an important element of the closer working relationship we want to see between prison and probation. We want whenever possible to prepare people serving prison sentences for jobs when they are released.

Q. **Are there further steps we need to take to strengthen provision for basic skills?**

Q. **How can we provide basic skills to people already in work?**

Employability skills for unemployed people

3.27 Many people who have been unemployed for some time missed out on foundation skills earlier in their lives. That is why education and training are central to all four options in the New Deal for young people aged 18 to 24. For some - primarily those without NVQ level 2 or equivalent - the route to employability will lie in full-time education and training. They will be able to study for up to a year towards a qualification, or units which can go towards one. Study above NVQ level 2 will also be possible where it is linked to getting a job.

3.28 We plan to extend the New Deal to those aged over 25 who are long-term unemployed. We have already announced that for those aged 25 and over who have been unemployed for two years or more, we propose to amend the Jobseeker's Allowance (JSA) rules so that they can also study full-time for up to a year without having to be available for employment in term time. In the five prototype Employment Zones, people aged over 25 who have, in the main, been unemployed for a year, will receive tailored training and education to meet their needs. We are also running Workskill pilot projects to help us see how changes in benefit rules on education and training can assist people to get and retain a job and we will review the JSA rules on education and training.

Skills for young people

3.29 The earlier we get the foundations right, the better the chances of developing a learning culture in the workplace. Employers and young people have reacted enthusiastically to Modern Apprenticeships which include the higher level and technician skills needed by modern manufacturing. There are currently over 110,000 Modern Apprentices. We will make available an additional 10,000 Modern Apprenticeships in 1998-99, with a particular emphasis on young people aged 19 or over, on areas in which there are skill shortages, and on encouraging take-up by small and medium size enterprises. Employers will be invited to bid for these. Focusing on the older age group will help those wishing to build on their achievements under National Traineeships, or who missed out on the vocational route at an earlier age. We will work with employers in developing the new National Traineeships.

Developing technician skills

3.30 Modern Apprenticeships and further education are now prioritising skills and underpinning knowledge in engineering, manufacturing, office systems and information technology in response to demand. An increasing number of people and firms are looking to upgrade their technician skills, and responding to this will be a priority for the University for Industry, TECs and further education colleges. We will encourage providers to seek partnerships with local businesses, in particular to ensure that the technology available matches that used by firms.

Applying graduate and postgraduate skills

3.31 In the modern competitive world, a growing number of employers need staff with high level skills. One in three of new entrants to the labour market are graduates, and higher and further education institutions are increasingly

delivering courses for people already in work. There is now a greater emphasis on advanced management and other professional skills and qualifications. We have recently announced pilot studies, in four industrial sectors, of the new Graduate Apprenticeships, to be designed jointly by National Training Organisations and universities or colleges. We want to see continuing links between higher education and employers to ensure that suitable courses are available for postgraduates in the years ahead. The University for Industry will address professional development as part of its range of courses.

3.32 Research in universities underpins world-beating UK companies, with universities playing a major role in providing postgraduate training for research scientists. These scientists contribute to industrial success either through continuing university-based research or by doing research in companies.

Strengthening managerial skills

3.33 The skills of managers, owners and the self-employed are fundamental to an organisation's success. Managers need to be committed to their own learning as well as enabling and encouraging their staff to get involved. One sign of progress is the number of managers now studying for MBAs (Master of Business Administration): 30,000 compared to 18,000 four years ago. There has been an even sharper rise in the number of people working towards management NVQs and SVQs (Scottish Vocational Qualifications); 100,000 compared to 40,000 four years ago. We will work with the planned Management and Enterprise National Training Organisation, and others, to:

- encourage people working in the professions to develop management skills alongside their specialist ones;

- encourage managers in smaller firms to develop the new skills they will need as their organisations grow;

- develop the University for Industry's support for managers, including within small firms;

- improve the links between vocational and academic qualifications and study in management; and

- explore the value of a new management code, incorporating ethical and environmental responsibilities as well as a commitment to learning.

Support for skills

3.34 Employers will need support to transform learning in the workplace. Sources of support include:

- the new *National Training Organisations* - the employer-led bodies responsible for improving training in their sectors. We have approved requests from industry to establish 37 NTOs between May 1997 and January 1998. A key function of the NTOs will be to promote occupational standards and NVQs to businesses in their sector, driving up participation in learning at work. Over half of our medium-size and larger firms are involved with vocational qualifications, offering them to a total of 3.8 million workers. A recent CBI study showed that NVQs improve both the quality of management and the standards of in-house training;

- *Training and Enterprise Councils:* we propose to ask TECs to draw up integrated plans to develop the local workforce. We envisage that these plans will: link with TECs' work on the New Deal and on work-based training for young people and unemployed adults; cover their work with partners to integrate skills and training advice with Business Link support to firms; and be agreed with local authorities, colleges and universities. TECs will also provide feedback to the University for Industry about gaps in provision, skills trends and opportunities for further development;

- *further education colleges* whose traditional close links with local employers have been strengthened through work on NVQs and franchised provision on employers' premises; and

- *universities and higher education colleges* which increasingly play a major role in supporting local businesses on skills and technology transfer.

Q. Are these support mechanisms the right ones to help raise the level and quality of training in the workplace, and how do they fit in with Regional Development Agencies?

Q. Do they have the necessary 'purchase' to change culture and attitudes, or are more fundamental changes required?

Q. What should the future role of TECs be in supporting learning at work?

Q. **Do NTOs have sufficient leverage to raise the quantity and quality of training in their sectors?**

Q. **How can we ensure that local partners - including TECs, further and higher education, and local authorities - work together to support enterprises in improving learning?**

Priorities for early action

We propose to:

- establish Investors in People as the general standard for employers;

- set new targets for workplace learning;

- establish a Skills Task Force;

- encourage workplace partnership between employers, employees and their trade unions to promote learning;

- develop benchmarking of employers' investment in developing skills and the publication of more information on employers' investment in learning;

- require TECs to produce workforce development plans;

- build National Traineeships and Modern Apprenticeships as employers' preferred route to skills for their new recruits, and increase help with basic skills; and

- establish strong, employer-led National Training Organisations able to drive up participation and standards in learning at work.

Realising the Learning Age will require every part of the education and training system to make its contribution. The challenge is formidable, but the rewards will be great if we succeed.

4 Realising the Learning Age

Opening up access

4.1 In October 1997, the Prime Minister announced that the Government will provide for an extra 500,000 people in further and higher education by 2002. This pledge will allow more people to have the chance of a college or a university education and will extend educational opportunity to many people who would not otherwise have had the chance to learn.

4.2 This Chapter considers the role that the learning institutions and others supporting them will play in the Learning Age, and in particular how they can open up access for the many and not the few. We would welcome views on their contribution and on the support they will need in order to achieve the ambitious objectives we have set.

Supporting young people

4.3 Acquiring the learning habit early will help individuals to sustain it later in life. Our proposals for foundation learning have been set out in detail in the White Paper

Excellence in Schools. We want more young people to stay on in full-time education and training and achieve a qualification. No-one should be written off as a failure at the age of 16. This will take time, entail significant changes in attitudes and expectations, and require a major collective effort.

4.4 Our Investing in Young People (IiYP) strategy is a comprehensive approach aimed at young people who have not achieved while at school. It is designed to encourage all young people to continue studying so that they achieve, or are on the road to, a level 2 qualification (or higher if they are able). Schools will set targets for attainment of qualifications at the age of 16, with a wider range of vocational options and more work relevance in the curriculum. Through our introduction of a single school leaving date, all young people will have the chance to sit their GCSEs or other external examinations before they are able to leave school. IiYP will be supported by our New Start programme to re-motivate young people from the age of 14 who are disenchanted with learning.

4.5 For young people in work, we are legislating to give all 16 and 17 year-olds a statutory right to undertake education and training, with the support of their employer, to get to NVQ level 2. We are also introducing National Traineeships as a high quality work-based route to NVQ level 2, including key skills. We want all young people to plan their own learning, supported by a new National Record of Achievement and a Learning Card telling them about their entitlement to continue in learning post-16.

4.6 The Careers Service will help support young people in making informed choices and so help reduce the cost of bad decisions and subsequent drop-out from learning. From September 1998, we propose to require schools to run careers education programmes in Years 9 to 11. The earlier this work starts the better, and we will therefore encourage schools to widen awareness and raise aspirations from Year 7. The Qualifications and Curriculum Authority (QCA) will produce guidance for schools on developing careers education programmes.

4.7 We propose to concentrate individual careers guidance on those who are most at risk of losing their way. From this summer the priority for the Careers Service will be to follow-up, and keep in touch with, all 16 year-olds who are not in education and training. This will include finding new ways of involving parents and families in young people's career thinking and planning, and providing more help for those who are hardest to help.

4.8 To support this work, we are investing an additional £6 million in the Careers Service in 1998-99, as well as making extra funds available through the Careers Service

to schools and further education colleges for staff development.

4.9 The Youth Service will also be involved in supporting our strategy for young people. Some parts of the Youth Service are already attracting and helping many young people who have failed in, or have been failed by, more formal education. We want to see this built upon in partnership with the voluntary sector and others as a priority for the Service. We are undertaking a national audit of provision in every local authority in England. Drawing on this, we will look to put the Youth Service on a stronger statutory footing and ensure that voluntary youth networks and local authorities come together to provide for young people in an imaginative way.

4.10 This is a challenging programme. It forms part of the Government's wider strategy to restore hope, motivation and the opportunity for sustained employment to a generation of young people who have lost them. It links directly with our wider Welfare to Work programme, and with the reform of the youth justice system which aims to nip in the bud the drift into crime following failure at school. An important contribution to this is to help young offenders, as with other young people, gain literacy, numeracy and other key skills.

Q. How should the Careers Service best develop providing advice and guidance to young people. In particular, what should the balance be between universal provision, targeted help for some young people, and work with adults?

Q. In what ways can the Youth Service best support the Government's strategy for young people?

Q. How could the University for Industry support the Investing in Young People strategy?

Further education and the Kennedy Report

4.11 Further education colleges will play a key role in educating both young people and adults. Young people aged between 16 and 18 make up 20 per cent of the four million students in further education. The majority are adults over 18, most of whom study part-time. Student numbers have grown by a quarter in the last four years, while unit costs have fallen by 12 per cent.

4.12 Further education has demonstrated innovation and flexibility in response to new demands from individuals and businesses. Many colleges have worked imaginatively to improve access, operating across a number of sites and working collaboratively with employers, LEAs, community organisations and private training providers. The sector also has an excellent track record in reaching disadvantaged people, helping to reduce social exclusion and promoting employability.

4.13 More 16 and 17 year olds study full-time in further education colleges than at school. We will look at how recognition can be given to this, including issues surrounding funding. We will promote greater co-operation between schools and colleges in sharing resources and in providing greater choice. In some places there is also potential for greater efficiency through rationalisation of provision and facilities, harnessing competition and making progress through local partnerships. The development of a collaborative network of tertiary education is a long-term objective of the Government.

4.14 *Learning Works* - the report of the Committee on Widening Participation chaired by Baroness Kennedy and published last year - set out a clear vision of how to build on this record to transform individual and national performance. The report, commissioned by the FEFC, emphasises that providers, particularly colleges, should seek out groups with low participation and people who have not achieved their full potential. It sees further education as the key to breaking the vicious circle of poor economic performance and an inadequate standard of living.

4.15 The challenge facing us is great. 62 per cent (21 million people) of the adult population of working age do not have a level 3 qualification - the minimum to which the Kennedy report believes people should aspire in future. 40 per cent of the adult population of working age (14 million people) do not have a level 2 qualification. Many people's life experiences and knowledge should entitle them to recognition and accreditation which they have not received in the past.

4.16 The Government endorses the Kennedy report's vision. It sets out a radical vision which we must pursue over the years ahead. Our detailed response to the report is being published alongside this consultation paper. We agree that further education will be at the centre of widening participation, together with adult and residential community education and non-traditional approaches. Widening participation, however, is not enough on its own. Students have a right to high standards of teaching so that they can achieve. Our proposals for raising standards in further education are set out in Chapter Five.

4.17 Meeting the challenge will take time but we have already made a start. We have announced additional funding totalling £100 million for further education to provide for up to 80,000 additional students over the next year. The great majority will be drawn from the educationally disadvantaged population.

Q. How can we make sure that wider participation is achieved in expanding further education?

Q. Have we identified the main priorities for further education?

Learning at home and in the community

4.18 Community, adult and family learning will be essential in the Learning Age. It will help improve skills, encourage economic regeneration and individual prosperity, build active citizenship, and inspire self-help and local development. We propose to draw on the considerable experience of community development projects to help us see how leadership and involvement in the neighbourhood can be part of the learning process and how community education can support such self-help. The Committee on Education for Citizenship and the Teaching of Democracy, chaired by Professor Bernard Crick, will be exploring these issues as part of its remit.

4.19 Voluntary and community organisations, for example tenants' and residents' groups, mother and toddler groups, environmental organisations, and bodies like the Workers' Educational Association and residential colleges, are also resources for promoting community learning. We will support innovative work with charitable trusts and companies which are keen to contribute. We are proposing to set up an Adult and Community Learning Fund to sustain and encourage new schemes locally that help men and women gain access to education, including literacy and numeracy. We will make £5 million available next year through the Basic Skills Agency and NIACE (the National Institute for Adult and Continuing Education), and will look to match this with contributions from trusts, charities, companies and private donors.

4.20 We would welcome views on how to build on the many ways in which community learning can take place. Over one million people take adult education classes. They enhance retirement for many people and there is a link with the proposal in the Government's Green Paper *Our Healthier Nation* (Cm 3854) to set up healthy living centres funded from National Lottery money. The University for Industry will also have a part to play in supporting innovation.

4.21 We want to encourage families to learn together. The National Year of Reading will help in this, and our new Early Excellence Centres will promote parenting, family learning, and adult education and training, supported by childcare.

4.22 We welcome Professor Fryer's Advisory Group report, *Learning for the Twenty-First Century*, and look forward to the Group's further advice as part of the consultation process on how this area of learning can be developed.

Q. What further steps would most practically assist learning at home and in the community?

Q. How could the University for Industry support community learning?

Higher education and the Dearing Report

4.23 Higher education, offering high quality and high standards, has a central role to play in the Learning Age. It enables young people to complete their initial education up to the highest levels and equips them for work. It provides for an increasing number of mature entrants both as full-time and part-time students. It works with employers to provide them and their employees with the skills they will increasingly need, and with high quality strategic and applied research which benefits both the economy and our national life.

4.24 Our record in winning major science awards is proof of the excellence of our universities and UK higher education's information technology network - JANET and SuperJANET - is among the most advanced in the world. We want more people to have the chance to experience the excellence of higher education for themselves. Our universities make a major contribution to the country's research effort. They produce and disseminate new knowledge and understanding, both for their own sake and for use in developing and exploiting applications and technologies which enhance the UK's competitiveness, prosperity and quality of life. The Government is committed to maintaining a world-class science and research base.

4.25 We must build on the expertise of our universities to ensure that the most advanced knowledge and techniques are transferred into competitive economic success, including at regional and local levels. This involves universities and colleges sharing their expertise with industry and services in a pioneering way. An example of this is Technopole run by a partnership involving Sheffield's two universities, the city's science and technology parks, local industry and research and testing organisations. The Technopole network is helping firms throughout the UK and abroad to solve metals and materials manufacturing problems.

4.26 Universities and higher education colleges educated 2.8 million students in 1996-97. Less than a quarter were from the group which used to be the mainstay of the old universities - young people studying full-time for a qualification. Of those pursuing a qualification, 64 per cent were mature students and 37 per cent part-timers. Nearly one million people enrol with higher education institutions not to gain a qualification, but to meet a particular skill need or fill a gap in their knowledge, or just because they want to learn. Higher education is a major contributor to local, regional and national economic growth and regeneration.

4.27 The Government remains committed to the principle that anyone who has the capability for higher education should have the opportunity to benefit from it. The role of universities and colleges in lifelong learning will be reinforced by lifting the present cap on numbers. The additional numbers in higher education, which will increase participation by mature students and young people, will allow us both to meet the expected demand from young people and widen access to higher education. We expect more than half the additional places to be taken by mature students, including those who did not achieve traditional A level qualifications at school. Some will join from special access courses organised jointly with further education colleges, and many will seek part-time degrees. We will monitor take-up by mature students and look at the use of access funds to support them.

4.28 We wish universities, higher and further education to be beacons of learning in their local communities. At today's participation rates, 60 per cent of school-leavers can expect to enter higher education at some time in their lives. We propose that higher education should play an even bigger part in future by:

- providing more places to meet demand;

- offering a wide range of courses up to post-graduate level;

- ensuring high standards so as to enhance the employability of graduates;

- improving participation by offering opportunities later in life to those who missed out first time around;

- contributing more to the economy and being more responsive to the needs of business;

- collaborating effectively with other institutions, other learning providers and with the world of work; and

- making itself more accessible by exploiting new technology and flexible delivery with facilities available at times convenient to students.

4.29 The future development of higher education was the subject of a report by the National Committee of Inquiry into Higher Education, chaired by Sir Ron (now Lord) Dearing, published in July 1997. The Report - *Higher Education in the learning society* - emphasised the key role that higher education has to play in helping deliver the Learning Age. The National Committee of Inquiry into Higher Education was set up to make recommendations on how the purposes, shape, structure, size and funding of higher education, including support for students, should develop to meet the needs of the United Kingdom over the next 20 years. It also dealt with staff training and development, qualifications and standards, research, information technology, and governance. The Government has already responded to its recommendations on funding and student support, and our comprehensive response is published in a separate policy statement alongside this consultation paper.

Opening up access

4.30 Our priority is to reach out and include those who have been under-represented in higher education. They include people with disabilities and young people from semi-skilled or unskilled family backgrounds and from poorer localities. Although 54 per cent of young people from professional and managerial homes go on to higher education, only 17 per cent of those from semi-skilled and unskilled family backgrounds do so. Their relatively low participation results mainly from under-attainment at earlier stages of education. We have already started to tackle this, and our plans for further education will enable more people to go on to higher education.

4.31 We also need to identify the reasons that lead some young people not to consider higher education; for example, why some ethnic minority groups are under-represented as are women in some important disciplines. While men and women from ethnic minorities are generally better represented in higher education than in the general population, Bangladeshi women and Afro-Caribbean men remain under-represented, as do men and women from the most deprived parts of the country.

4.32 We will particularly encourage better links between schools and further education colleges in disadvantaged areas and universities or higher education colleges. We want students from families without a background of going to university to have more support and encouragement to stay in education after 16, raise their sights, and fulfil their potential by progressing to higher education. We are discussing with Oxford and Cambridge the part they can play in widening access.

4.33 The Dearing Committee made a number of recommendations on under-represented groups which we wish to see implemented. They include: targeting additional funding at universities and colleges with a commitment to widening participation and plans to improve access; joint further and higher education projects to address low expectations and low achievement and to promote progression to higher education; and incentives from funding bodies for the enrolment of students from particularly disadvantaged localities. The Higher Education Funding Council for England has allocated £2 million in 1998/99 and £4 million in 1999/2000 to support such projects, and is considering significant changes in the way it funds teaching to reward institutions committed to widening access and outreach. We will be discussing with HEFCE further steps to achieve a substantial change, building on the standards agenda we are pursuing in schools and colleges.

4.34 Many higher education institutions have a tradition of outreach programmes for adults which provide valuable opportunities for mature students to take courses, which do not lead to degrees, on a part-time basis. Some are designed to help adults without qualifications reach the necessary level to enrol for a degree, giving them a hand-up to higher education. Other courses lead to certificates or diplomas which are self-standing and enable people, who in most cases have not had the benefit of higher education, to gain from the experience of study at a higher education institution without the greater commitment of enrolling for a degree. This work is a vital contribution to lifelong learning, and we will expect the Funding Councils, universities and colleges of higher education to attach high priority to its continuation.

4.35 Our aims for higher education are to achieve wider access and high standards. We have already provided an extra £125 million for 1998-99 to preserve and enhance quality, and an additional £40 million to improve access and help disadvantaged groups. This includes £4 million to make a start on growth in the number of places on diploma courses, mainly in further education. This action has started to address the funding crisis facing higher education and to focus resources more effectively.

The Open University (OU) success story......

The Open University, based on open entry and supported high quality open learning, has shown how much can be achieved by adults of all backgrounds and ages.

More than two million people have studied with the OU since it started. 200,000 will do so this year, including more than half of all part-time UK undergraduate students. The OU has increased access and extended opportunities to those who might not otherwise have entered higher education. Two thirds of OU students are aged between 30 and 49; three-quarters are in full-time employment; half are women; some 5,000 have disabilities; and almost half of OU graduates had fathers who were in manual occupations. Over one-third of the OU's undergraduate students did not possess normal entry requirements on joining, but an impressively high percentage go forward to achieve credits and qualifications or continue learning in other institutions. The OU is one the UK's great education success stories.

Getting more young people to think about a university place.......

HiPACT is a national network of 16 higher education institutions aiming to motivate young people in schools without a strong tradition of entry into higher education. Businesses and other organisations can support the work of HiPACT.

Under HiPACT's Target Achievement Programme (TAP) institutions have agreed to give special consideration to applicants from participating schools and, in many cases, reserve conditional offers at achievable grades which recognise that their grades alone may not fully reflect their potential. HiPACT works with other organisations to help co-ordinate motivational activities including summer schools and university visits. A survey of TAP projects showed that it can transform attitudes to higher and further education and helps motivate even those pupils who decide not to apply to university.

4.36 We propose to explore with voluntary and statutory bodies how best to improve access to further and higher education and training for students with disabilities and special educational needs, including severe learning difficulties. We will launch our New Deal for disabled people and help students with disabilities in higher education, including by abolishing the means-test for Disabled Students Allowances. We will build on the *Inclusive Learning* report produced by Professor John Tomlinson's Committee. The FEFC has already committed £5 million over three years for a quality initiative for staff development and an additional £5 million in 1998-99 for students with learning difficulties and disabilities. We also want to make sure that all programmes for improving quality include people with disabilities and learning difficulties, as proposed in our Green Paper *Excellence for all children* (Cm 3785).

Q. Have we identified the right priorities to meet the needs of people with disabilities or learning difficulties?

Libraries

4.37 The public library service holds an enormous range of educational material and has the potential to deliver information and learning to people of all ages and backgrounds, right across the country. The Learning Age will be supported by the development of new information and communication technology within libraries.

4.38   We have already announced that we will provide £50 million from the Lottery to provide digital content for libraries. Further proposals for the development of the public libraries IT network, which will be an integral part of the National Grid for Learning, will be published shortly.

Using libraries to get people learning......

When Shibani Basu was appointed as community librarian in Merton, she realised that local Asian women made relatively little use of the library service (although they did bring their children). The library was a safe and respectable place to meet and therefore a potentially important resource for them, so the Asian Women's Association was set up in 1988. Membership now stands at over 250.

Activities include workshops, discussions, lectures, arts and crafts sessions, health education and assertiveness courses. Meetings and events are carefully timed - afternoons, for example, are much better than evenings when the women often have family responsibilities. Members not only learn a wide range of skills through the meetings, but have in some cases gone on to take training courses (for example, on running a small business).

The creative industries

4.39 To help improve economic performance in the creative industries, the Government has established a task force, chaired by the Secretary of State for Culture, Media and Sport, to take a broad view of the cultural economy. A key activity will be to identify and promote the contribution lifelong learning can make to the sector's performance.

4.40 The creative industries have an educational dimension in their own right. People learn from visits to the theatre, cinema, art galleries and museums. We also need to nurture the creative spirit in education itself. We are establishing an advisory group on creativity and innovation, chaired by Professor Ken Robinson, to look at how this can be encouraged in both schools and further and higher education.

Science and manufacturing

4.41 Science has an important contribution to make to the Learning Age. An understanding and appreciation of science is of great value throughout the world of work and also within the home and wider community. Science is also at the cutting edge of many of the new industries and products on which the UK's economic prosperity depends. Manufacturing remains essential to the United Kingdom's economic future, and it will need a continuing supply of highly-trained, skilled employees. Technician skills will be particularly important. For example, the use of information and communication technologies is leading to a rapid growth in demand for highly skilled maintenance technicians.

Working together

4.42 All of our proposals are aimed at improving the skills, creativity and employability of our people, young and old, and at promoting a fair society in which all have a stake. We cannot realise these goals unless we join together to do so. The Government's role will be to provide a lead so that everyone is clear about their responsibilities and focuses on setting and meeting agreed targets.

4.43 Local authorities will play a major role in helping to carry forward learning throughout life. Local authorities act as providers, co-ordinators and supporters of lifelong learning in many different ways. We will be consulting with the Local Government Association about how the contribution of local authorities can best be focused, including through Education Development Plans and strategic planning with other major partners.

Local action

4.44 Local challenges need local solutions. We will not lay down a blueprint from the centre. However, we do see three priorities for all areas and therefore propose:

- to ask TECs to develop local workforce development plans;

- to encourage sensible local planning. We will work with the FEFC, the Local Government Association and local partners to develop more coherent planning and funding arrangements in post-16 education. We will establish a new Collaboration Fund which will help further education colleges to work with each other, and with other post-16 providers, to develop more cost-effective and relevant provision;

- to encourage every community to develop its education potential, involving all types of learning institutions. We will consult on how to invite LEAs, further education and others to do this. We will want to draw on best practice including the current pilots funded by the FEFC following the Kennedy report.

4.45 We will continue to support the recent rapid growth in the numbers of towns, cities and other communities which have committed themselves to learning through work with the Learning Cities Network, and will explore how we can extend that support to smaller towns and rural communities.

4.46 As the University for Industry develops and the National Grid for Learning spreads progressively out from schools, local partnerships will be crucial to their effective impact on the ground. The development of local learning centres in communities, in institutions and at the workplace will be a key aspect of the University for Industry.

The Regions

4.47 The new Regional Development Agencies will play an important role - working with partners - in developing the Learning Age. In drawing up their economic strategies, RDAs will: help tackle skill shortages and identify future skill needs; support local partnerships through the Single Regeneration Budget Challenge Fund and integrate regeneration with economic development; engage further and higher education in their work; ensure that regional economic and labour market trends influence decisions about training and careers advice and guidance; and

design inward investment packages, including support for learning.

Working internationally

4.48 We will aim to put our vision of the Learning Age at the heart of thinking in the European Union. Following the European Year of Lifelong Learning in 1996, the UK Presidency in the first half of 1998 is an important opportunity to link the need for learning to employability. We want to work with our European partners to ensure that the new generation of EU education, training and youth programmes from the year 2000 onwards reflect this. We will host a wide range of events to raise the profile of lifelong learning during our Presidency. We will also promote initiatives aimed at young people, including:

- developing measures to benefit apprentices and other trainees;

- supporting the very large number of UK organisations funded under the EU Telematics Education and Training programme;

- hosting our Second Chance School aimed at bringing people back into learning; and

- agreeing a new European Voluntary Service programme for young people.

4.49 The European Social Fund (ESF) and other European initiatives make a major contribution to lifelong learning. In particular, the ADAPT Programme has provided support for trans-national pilot projects focusing on training delivery within small and medium-size enterprises. The ESF has also allocated £1.3 billion for the period 1997-99 to the Objective 3 programme which targets disadvantaged groups and funds projects to help increase their skill and qualification level.

4.50 The Government is determined to make the best use of potential European funding for lifelong learning. This includes:

- agreeing a new programme under Objective 4 to use European Social Fund (ESF) money to support our policies including the University for Industry, Investors in People and individual learning accounts;

- using funds drawn from elsewhere in the European Social Fund to tackle skills development, outreach and investment in learning-poor communities;

- negotiating to use ADAPT programme money to provide development projects with a trans-national flavour for the University for Industry; and planning to allow projects for 16-19 year olds and under the New Deal to be able to draw in ESF money to increase their range of activity; and

- negotiating to ensure that the new generation of EU education, training and youth programmes from 2000 onwards offer coherent and strategic support for lifelong learning.

Q. What areas should the next generation of EU programmes support?

We propose to:

- increase numbers in higher and further education by 500,000 by 2002 and improve access;

- work with higher and further education to implement the recommendations of the Dearing and Kennedy reports;

- raise attainment and participation of 16-19 year-olds through Investing in Young People and enhancing the contributions of the Careers and Youth Services;

- expand work-based training for young people particularly through the Modern Apprenticeship programme;

- strengthen learning in the family and in communities, and establish an Adult and Community Learning Fund;

- improve provision specifically for people with disabilities or learning difficulties;

- establish local planning for lifelong learning by all the key players;

- establish the Regional Development Agencies with a focus on support for lifelong learning; and

- put our vision of the Learning Age at the heart of thinking in Europe.

Chapter 5

The UK must aim for world-class standards in the Learning Age.

5 | Ensuring Standards Quality and Accountability

Raising standards

5.1 Wherever and whenever people and businesses choose to learn, they should be entitled to high quality learning that:

- delivers what it promises;

- gets them to their goals; and

- takes them as high up the ladder of achievement as they are able to go.

5.2 This will mean a major drive to raise standards. This drive will parallel the approach for schools set out in *Excellence in Schools*. In post-16 education and training this will involve:

- meeting individual learners' needs and aspirations;

- promoting high quality teaching;

- setting, publishing and meeting targets for improving achievement over time;

- identifying and dealing with weaknesses;

- having objective external assessment; and

- ensuring good value for money .

Further education

5.3 High standards must continue to be a priority for further education. There are many examples of high quality, responsive and accessible courses, and in some colleges, performance and results are outstanding. However, in others there is a persistent problem of low achievement and poor retention rates.

5.4 We propose, working with colleges, the Further Education Funding Council and the Further Education Development Agency (FEDA) to:

- get all colleges to adopt a rigorous approach to standards, with systematic assessment and target setting. Each college should set annual targets to improve retention and achievement, and publish the results;

- ensure better teaching. Our aim is that all new teachers in further education should hold, or within two years of appointment have begun, a recognised initial teacher training qualification. This would apply both to full-time teachers and those with a substantial part-time commitment. To provide a framework for this and for continuing professional development, further education will have established a National Training Organisation for the sector by the end of the year;

- get the right balance between full and part-time tutors and lecturers, so that colleges are flexible enough to cope with rapid change, but also have sufficient continuity to secure their objectives;

- promote improvements in college management. Inspection reveals this is crucial to high standards, yet management training in the sector is patchy and of uneven quality. We look forward to the national framework for management development based on standards of best business practice being completed by the summer to provide a coherent structure for the training of college managers.

5.5 High standards must also apply to accountability. Colleges' independence should not stand in the way of openness and responsiveness to the local community. The Kennedy committee commented on the current lack of formal arrangements for community involvement, and accountability in its widest sense has been lacking. Since the incorporation of further education colleges there have been concerns about the style of working and remoteness of governing bodies. Some have encouraged a confrontational management style which is unacceptable for publicly funded bodies.

5.6 We therefore propose to consult shortly on proposals for detailed changes to the statutory framework for college governing bodies to ensure this accountability and openness. These changes will cover: representation for the local authority, staff, students and community interests (including parents where there is a significant proportion of students aged 16 to 18); open decision-making; annual reports; clear and open procedures for the appointment and accountability of senior management and for dealing with complaints; and codes of conduct governing the appointment of governors, their conduct and interests.

Q. **What are your views on our proposal for a recognised initial teacher training qualification in further education?**

Q. **Are the right issues being addressed in relation to accountability?**

5.7 Many LEAs provide imaginative and high quality adult education, often in partnership with other parts of local government, colleges or voluntary organisations. Others do not. LEAs are required to review the quality of adult education in institutions which they maintain or assist. Eight in ten LEAs use the self-assessment techniques recommended by the Office for Standards in Education (OFSTED): we expect all LEAs to do so. We will consult FEFC and OFSTED about ways of building on their current informal co-operation and develop proposals for joint work and some experimental work next year.

5.8 We will ask the Basic Skills Agency, the FEFC Inspectorate and OFSTED to work together and with others such as the Training Inspectorate to improve literacy and numeracy provision. This will include the use of the Basic Skills Agency's Quality Mark, and the use of benchmarks, targets and performance indicators, as well as reviewing standards of teaching and the use of materials.

Q. What approaches to improving quality will be most effective for adult education?

TECs and their providers

5.9 While the majority of TEC-funded training is of high quality, the action of some providers is cause for concern. In the worst cases, there has been evidence of fraud and misuse of resources, the use of unqualified and untrained staff, and unreliable assessment of qualifications. Such practices will be rooted out. We will be discussing with those concerned measures to improve the qualifications and competence of trainers. We have set up the Training Standards Council to supervise a Training Inspectorate which will drive up the standards of training funded through TECs. Inspection will be reinforced by mandatory self-assessment by providers.

5.10 The inter-TEC comparison tables show that TECs have become more effective. Many providers are working hard to improve standards. However, there is still wide variation between the best and the rest. To improve standards, we will work with the TEC National Council (TNC) and individual TECs to:

- introduce new licensing arrangements so that all TECs follow the internationally recognised Business Excellence Model;

- share best practice more effectively; and

- reduce the costs of administration and bureaucracy so releasing resources to improve the quality of training.

5.11 The TEC National Council has developed a framework for local accountability: adherence to its principles is a requirement of TECs' contract with the Government. This emphasises the importance of openness and transparency in:

- the selection of Board members;

- being seen to act effectively in the interests of the local community;

- being open about performance and about TECs' employment and financial policies; and

- dealing with customers, partners and suppliers.

5.12 We propose to make changes to the eligibility criteria for TEC directors. These will ensure that boards better reflect local communities and enhance accountability, while TECs remain employer-led bodies. We will also expect all TECs to appoint directors able to reflect the wider interests of the workforce and locally elected decision makers.

Q. Are there further steps needed to improve TEC accountability and effectiveness?

Q. What should be the priorities for the new Training Inspectorate?

A consistent approach to improving quality

5.13 Effective internal quality assurance systems, combined with regular independent inspections against a consistent framework of standards, are critical to raising quality and achievement and reducing drop-out rates. We propose now to build on the best practice which already exists and harmonise post-16 inspection arrangements across schools, further education colleges, LEAs' adult education and training providers. We will work with inspectors and providers and consult widely to develop a national framework and common procedures and marking systems. We propose to publish appropriate performance indicators and targets for individual providers.

Q. What are the most appropriate means of ensuring consistent inspection arrangements?

Q. Should we make provision for dealing with failing post-16 institutions as we have done with schools?

Higher education

5.14 Our aims for higher education are to achieve wider access and high standards. We have already provided £125 million for 1998-99 to preserve and enhance quality, and an additional £40 million to improve access. The Dearing Committee set out a new emphasis on quality and standards, designed to ensure that students who commit themselves to higher education are well taught and helped to succeed, and emerge with awards whose value is known and undisputed in the market places of the UK and the world. Our new funding system gives students the right to demand better quality of teaching and greater attention to their needs.

5.15 The higher education sector has responded positively to Dearing's recommendations and will be pursuing them. We attach great importance to the continued drive to improve standards and quality across teaching, research, and qualifications in higher education. The Government will monitor progress made in this area to assure the quality of teaching, the maintenance and raising of standards and the way that institutions respond to national policy.

5.16 We also think there should be a more direct link between institutions' funding and the quality and standards of teaching and learning. We believe that teaching in higher education deserves a higher profile in relation to research than it has had in the past. We welcome the Higher Education Funding Councils' consultation on the criticism there has been of the research assessment exercise. The Government would like to see a process for assessing the quality of research which enhances quality and innovation and which is open to a greater number of influences than peer review, drawing on research expertise from outside UK universities where this is appropriate and can be done in a cost-effective way.

5.17 The funding bodies should identify ways of rewarding the best in teaching and learning and successful outreach to the disadvantaged or under-represented. We also see the need to build up the standards and professional status of teachers in higher education. Central to achieving these changes will be the new Institute for Learning and Teaching in Higher Education recommended by Dearing, which the Government expects to be established as soon as possible. This will complement the work of the General Teaching Council for teachers in schools and the proposed NTO for Further Education.

5.18 The quality of teaching can be improved by making more widely available the work of outstanding teachers, and students should have the chance of hearing outstanding lecturers on film, video or via broadcasting. We will invite the Institute for Learning and Teaching in Higher Education, when it is established, to consider how this can be done.

5.19 Governing bodies have an important role in ensuring that universities and higher education colleges are accountable and effective. The Dearing committee's view was that universities and higher education colleges have responded to stakeholders' expectations of increased transparency, probity, accountability and efficiency, but that further action was needed. We expect to see sustained progress and will monitor the situation in order to assess whether the Dearing Committee's recommendations should be revisited.

Q. Is the action we propose sufficient to secure improved quality and standards in higher education?

Priorities for early action

We propose to:

- secure major improvements in retention and achievement in further education;

- work with TECs to raise standards and effectiveness;

- work with OFSTED, the FEFC and LEAs to set and monitor standards for adult education arranged through LEAs;

- improve and harmonise inspection arrangements post-16 and the monitoring of performance across schools, further education and training, including setting in place an independent Training Inspectorate; and

- monitor the implementation of the Dearing committee's recommendations on quality and standards within higher education.

Qualifications in the Learning Age should meet the needs of people and uphold standards. They must value both academic and vocational achievement, and be easily understood, flexible, and widely recognised.

6 | Recognising Achievement

The value of qualifications

6.1 Qualifications are a means to an end, and not an end in themselves. Once seen as being purely for young people, today qualifications give signals about our employability and allow us to progress. They tell individuals and employers what is needed to achieve a given standard or skill. They help motivate people to stick with learning. They provide step-by-step progress through education and training, thus helping people to move forward or change direction in their careers.

6.2 Qualifications should allow people to take small steps and choose combinations of learning that suit them, while being recognised by employers and society as a whole. We must also acknowledge that not everyone who learns needs or wants a qualification.

6.3 Our aims for qualifications are to:

- guarantee and maintain high standards;

- ensure they require, and give credit for, both breadth and depth of study for those aged 16-19;

- provide for adult learners and encourage lifelong learning;

- raise awareness of their importance and availability; and

- make the system more easily understood.

6.4 A wide variety of qualifications is currently available. The main national qualifications - classified by level and broad equivalence - are set out in the chart overleaf.

Qualifications explained..........

Foundation/Level 1	National Vocational Qualification (NVQ) level 1
	General National Vocational Qualification (GNVQ) Foundation Level
	5 GCSE Grades D-G
Intermediate/Level 2	NVQ level 2
	GNVQ Intermediate Level
	5 GCSE Grades A*-C
Advanced/Level 3	NVQ level 3
	GNVQ Advanced Level
	2 GCE A levels
Higher/Levels 4 and 5	NVQ levels 4 and 5
	Higher National Certificates and Diplomas
	Degrees and Post-graduate Qualifications

Note: NVQs test the abilities needed in particular occupations. GNVQs are courses which cover a broad occupational area.

Coherence and quality

6.5 In order to protect standards and simplify the qualifications system, we have established the Qualifications and Curriculum Authority in England. The QCA will:

- develop a framework for all nationally recognised qualifications (other than those awarded by higher education institutions) so that people know what their qualification means;

- accredit awarding bodies, so that people can rely on the quality of their qualification. This will be helped by the formation of three unitary awarding bodies for 16-19 qualifications; and

- ensure that qualifications reflect the needs of industry and of higher education, working with the National Training Organisations and with the Quality Assurance Agency for higher education.

Qualifications for young people

6.6 We have already invited views on our commitment to broaden A levels and improve vocational qualifications for young people. Our recent consultation *Qualifying for Success* included proposals for a single overarching certificate which would become the benchmark for attainment at advanced level, giving credit for both breadth and depth of study. We believe that all young people should have the chance to show what they have achieved. We will be announcing shortly how we intend to proceed in the light of advice from the QCA.

Records of Achievement

6.7 We are already piloting a new approach to the national record of achievement in schools. But adults also need to be able to identify their needs, make plans to meet those needs and monitor their progress. Chapter 2 sets out how we plan to explore ways of linking individual learning accounts and the planning and recording of achievement through smartcard technology. We will also develop a core of material for use by colleges, employers and private publishers, and work with them to produce systems that meet their needs and those of their customers.

Q. What form should a record of achievement take to maximise its use to learners and its relevance to employers?

Key skills

6.8 Young people and adults need certain skills to develop and maintain their employability. These are:

- working with other people;

- effective communication, including written skills;

- the ability to work with numbers;

- the use of information technology;

- developing learning skills; and

- problem-solving.

6.9 We want to enable young people and adults to gain these key skills in higher education, colleges and the workplace, although adults may not always want to gain a formal qualification. These skills can be learnt throughout life and to any level. They are as relevant on the shop floor as they are in the boardroom. There is merit in seeing communications, numeracy and IT as basic skills - essential for all - up to level 2 and in seeing key skills as the development of these and the others we have mentioned beyond that stage.

6.10 The Dearing committee on higher education recommended that communications, numeracy, the use of information technology and 'learning how to learn' should be part of all higher education programmes. We are working on this proposal with higher education and employer bodies and will fund a number of pilot projects. We are also looking at how work experience within higher education could help those who are not undertaking a vocational degree. This will assist us in promoting enterprise, innovation, self-motivation and job creation.

Q. How might we encourage the development of key skills for adults; through the use of qualifications being developed for 16-19 year olds, or through less formal or more varied means?

Q **Should we develop a firm notion of information technology as a basic skill? Would a firm distinction between the basic skills below level 2 and key skills at that level and beyond be useful?**

Qualifications for adult learners

6.11 Whether learners get public funding or are investing their own money, they deserve qualifications which meet high national standards. We propose to use powers in the Education Act 1997 to ensure that this is the case. The QCA will assure the quality of all nationally recognised qualifications and their awarding bodies.

6.12 The range of qualifications available at levels 2 and 3 - GCSEs, A levels, NVQs and GNVQs - are taken by some adults currently. We want to encourage more to do so. We propose to examine how qualifications targeted at adults can:

- be taken through a wide variety of methods of learning;

- be taken in small sections;

- offer a very wide variety of skills and subject matter; and

- stimulate the acquisition of basic and key skills.

6.13 Such qualifications should recognise experience and achievement in work, and through other voluntary and family activities. Recording such achievement can be a powerful stimulus to learning. We propose that the qualification system should be developed to recognise that learning can take place in many different forms, and that it may not always be appropriate for everyone to be pushed along the same qualifications 'tramlines'.

6.14 We will develop and promote National Vocational Qualifications which recognise the skills that people have attained at work. Available as units, they have been growing in popularity. With the newly established industry-led National Training Organisations and the QCA, we propose to ensure that individual NVQs meet the needs of individuals, changing skill requirements in industry and greater workforce flexibility. We also wish to develop the learning requirements of individual NVQs. NVQs will continue to be the cornerstone of Modern Apprenticeships and National Traineeships. We will also examine how far the NVQ system encourages adults to move up from level to level.

6.15 Many adults returning to learning want to take small steps. A full national qualification may not be the right goal for them to start with. We will be introducing a range of new entry level or 'starter' qualifications, aimed at those for whom foundation qualifications may be too daunting. We may need to go further. Many (including the Fryer and Kennedy committees) have called for a system in which people - particularly those taking the first steps back to education - can build up recognition for bits of learning at a time.

6.16 It may be possible to develop, within further education, a system of commonly understood credits as currently happens with arrangements for access to higher education for adult learners. This would be aimed at those undertaking courses which prepare for full qualifications. People could build up skills and knowledge bit by bit, as they needed it and when they could afford the time and investment. This would not prevent people from studying a particular unit even if they were not seeking a full qualification.

Q. Is a system of credit accumulation a sensible goal? What issues need to be addressed in establishing it?

Qualifications in higher education

6.17 We propose that a national framework for higher education qualifications should be introduced, as recommended by the Dearing committee. We look to the responsible bodies, including the Quality Assurance Agency for Higher Education, to maintain progress on the establishment of such a framework.

6.18 The main elements should be in place by 2000. We want to see a national Credit Accumulation and Transfer system*, to underpin the qualifications framework, and more 'stopping-off points', separately accredited, during higher education. This is so that people can build up blocks of qualifications over time and know what particular blocks of learning are worth.

6.19 We do not think that a case has been made for introducing GNVQs at levels 4 and 5. We will therefore look to the QCA and the Quality Assurance Agency for Higher Education to bring existing qualifications within the new post-16 and higher education frameworks in ways which are readily understood by individuals and employers and which promote comparability.

Q. Do you support the development of a Credit Accumulation and Transfer system for higher education?

Priorities for early action

We propose to:

- improve the accessibility of NVQs and maintain standards;

- start to bring a full range of nationally recognised qualifications within a coherent and comprehensible structure;

- start work on new ways of encouraging people to take their first steps back into learning (for example, through new entry level qualifications);

- allow qualifications to be combined more easily and explore the idea of a national framework of unit recognition for this purpose;

- support the development by universities and colleges of new ways for adults to plan their learning and record their achievement; and

- support the development by universities and colleges of a broad, consistent and easily understood national framework for higher education qualifications.

*CAT Schemes allow students to break away from the traditional model where a degree is acquired by studying for a set period at a single institution to a particular curriculum. Instead, credit points are awarded for individual modules and a final degree is achieved by accumulating sufficient credits. This transfers ownership to students, who can choose which modules to study and even mix full-time and part-time study over a convenient period

7 Consultation: how to respond

7.1 We believe that the proposals in this consultation paper will enable every part of society to benefit from the opportunities of the Learning Age: young people and people in retirement; people who are unemployed and those established in the workplace; people who need help with basic skills and those at post-graduate level; large and small businesses; employees and the self-employed; and the public and private sectors.

7.2 In summary, we will provide:

- as many **young people** as possible with the opportunity to achieve at least an NVQ level 2 qualification by the age of 19. We will re-motivate those who are disenchanted with learning through the New Start partnerships; give 16 and 17 year olds in employment a legal right to undertake education and training up to NVQ level 2; introduce National Traineeships; build on the success of Modern Apprenticeships; and support young people with a new National Record of Achievement and a Learning Card explaining their entitlement and the fact that it is free;

- new opportunities for people **in further and higher education**. They will help people to gain technician and higher level skills, including postgraduate development. The Government remains committed to the principle that anyone who has the capability for higher education should have the opportunity to benefit from it, and we will therefore lift the cap on student plans imposed by the last government;

- better opportunities for learning for **people at work** who want to raise their skills or re-train. The University for Industry will offer guidance and new ways to learn at home or at work using leading edge technology. Our new free-phone national helpline *Learning Direct* - open all day and in the evenings and on Saturday mornings - will offer people information about learning that is available. Individual learning accounts will help people take more responsibility for their own future by investing in their own education and training;

- help for **_people who need basic literacy and numeracy skills_** inside and outside the workforce. This will include new support and help through the Ufl; targeted individual learning accounts; our New Deals for unemployed people, lone parents and those with disabilities; and through wider family learning building on the success of our family literacy initiatives. As a start, we will invest £5m in 1998-99 in a new Adult and Community Education Fund to promote local innovation, especially in improving access and quality;

- support for **_businesses to secure the skills that they need_** to compete in the world. We will help organisations to meet the Investors in People standard in the training and development of their workforce; target the work of the Ufl particularly on the needs of small businesses and key sectors; support strong employer-led National Training Organisations in each major sector; promote better information about investment in training; and encourage further and higher education to build on the substantial contribution which they already make to addressing skills requirements and to improving UK competitiveness. We will set up a Skills Task Force to help ensure that we have the right skills required for the 21st Century; and

- encouragement for a **_modern partnership for learning in the workplace_** involving employers, employees and their trade unions. We will establish a £2m Employee Education Development Fund to support trade unions and other employee representative organisations to develop innovative workplace education.

Issues for consultation

7.3 We would welcome comments on all aspects of this Green Paper. The questions on which we would particularly like views are to be found in each Chapter, as well as being brought together below for ease of reference.

7.4 The main issues for consultation are:

Chapter 1

Are there other obstacles that people face beyond those set out in Chapter 1?

Do the steps outlined in paragraph 1.5 cover the main changes that are needed to make learning easier?

How can we raise awareness of what the Ufl has to offer individual learners and businesses?

Which people and businesses should the Ufl target in particular?

How can we best link the Ufl with individual learning accounts?

Should the Ufl focus exclusively on using new technology to deliver learning?

How can Learning Direct best fit in with local sources of advice?

How can Government and broadcasters maximise the contribution broadcasting can make to widening access to learning?

In what other ways can broadcasting and new information technologies support the Learning Age?

Chapter 2

Are our funding principles the right ones?

Are there further steps we should be taking to improve the balance of investment in learning between employers, individuals and the public purse?

Is it realistic to expect individuals or employers to invest more? If so, what form should this additional investment take?

How should learning accounts and the learning smartcard be developed to help people invest in and manage their own learning?

On what basis should the Government's contribution to up to one million learning accounts be allocated?

What will be needed to make learning accounts attractive to people, both financially and through the other advantages they will bring?

Should learning accounts be used in future to channel other forms of public support for learners?

What would be the most effective way of targeting financial support so that more young people from low-income families stay on in full-time education after 16?

Should support loans be made available to undergraduate students in their early 50s?

Are the steps we are taking sufficient to create a fair and effective system of student support?

Chapter 3

How should we develop the national framework for learning at work?

Are the measures we propose sufficient to meet the challenge?

What role could incentives play in encouraging investment by employers in workplace learning?

What contribution can businesses make to wider learning?

How can we encourage employers to offer more of their employees the chance to gain qualifications at work?

What measures are needed to ensure that people in work have the time they need to learn?

How can employers be encouraged to contribute to their employees' ILAs?

What more should be done to improve learning in small firms and organisations?

What steps could be taken to provide cover for small firms to allow employees to undertake training?

Are there any other steps that we could take to increase the take-up of Investors in People?

What measurements should be used to best assess investment in training?

How should this information be publicised?

Which priority skill areas should the National Skills Task Force focus on initially?

Are there further steps we need to take to strengthen provision for basic skills?

How can we provide basic skills to people already in work?

Are the current support mechanisms the right ones to help raise the level and quality of training in the workplace; and how do they fit in with Regional Development Agencies?

Do these mechanisms have the necessary 'purchase' to change culture and attitudes, or are more fundamental changes required?

What should the future role of TECs be in supporting learning at work?

Do NTOs have sufficient leverage to raise the quantity and quality of training in their sectors?

How can we ensure that local partners - including TECs, further and higher education, and local authorities - work together to support enterprises in improving learning?

Chapter 4

How should the Careers Service best develop providing advice and guidance to young people? In particular, what should the balance be between universal provision, targeted help for some young people, and work with adults?

In what ways can the Youth Service best support the Government's strategy for young people?

How could the University for Industry support the Investing in Young People strategy?

How can we make sure that wider participation is achieved in expanding further education?

Have we identified the main priorities for further education?

What further steps would most practically assist learning at home and in the community?

How could the University for Industry support community learning?

Have we identified the right priorities to meet the needs of people with disabilities or learning difficulties?

What areas should the next generation of EU programmes support?

Chapter 5

What are your views on our proposal for a recognised initial teacher training qualification in further education?

Are the right issues being addressed in relation to accountability in further education?

What approaches to improving quality will be most effective for adult education?

Are there further steps needed to improve TEC accountability and effectiveness?

What should be the priorities for the new Training Inspectorate?

What are the most appropriate means of ensuring consistent inspection arrangements?

Should we make provision for dealing with failing post-16 institutions as we have done with schools?

Is the action we propose sufficient to secure improved quality and standards in higher education?

Chapter 6

What form should a record of achievement take to maximise its use to learners and its relevance to employers?

How might we encourage the development of key skills for adults; through the use of qualifications being developed for 16-19 year olds, or through less formal or more varied means?

Should we develop a firm notion of information technology as a basic skill? Would a firm distinction between basic skills below level 2 and key skills at that level and beyond be useful?

Is a system of credit accumulation a sensible goal? What issues need to be addressed in establishing it?

Do you support the development of a Credit Accumulation and Transfer System for higher education?

7.5 Once all of the responses to this consultation document have been received, we will make them available and will draw on them in carrying forward the proposals set out in this paper.

How to respond

Copies

You can obtain copies of this Green Paper as a priced publication from the Stationery Office and its agents (for details, see the back cover). We have produced a summary version, which is being made widely available. This sets out the main proposals and issues for discussion. You may order copies, free of charge, from the special Learning Age helpline number given below. The summary contains a form which you can use to record your comments.

This consultation paper is available in English, Braille and on audio-cassette. The summary version is available in English, Bengali, Gujerati, Hindi, Punjabi, Urdu and Chinese, in Braille and on audio-cassette.

Access on the internet

This consultation paper is available via the Internet. The address is *http://www.lifelonglearning.co.uk.*

Consultation events

To promote discussion on the Green Paper, we are undertaking a full programme of consultation events. You can find out more about this by ringing the special Learning Age helpline.

Responding to the consultation paper

The deadline for sending in your views is 24 July 1998.

Please send your written or taped comments to: **Val Hewson, Department for Education and Employment, Individual Learning Division, Room E8, Moorfoot, Sheffield, S1 4PQ** or by fax to 0114 259 4148. Or, if you prefer it, please email them to *lifelong.learning@dfee.gov.uk.* Unfortunately, we cannot take individual comments by telephone or at our consultation events. Responses to the Green Paper will be made available to the public on request, unless you indicate that you wish your response to remain confidential.

The Learning Age Helpline

We have set up a special helpline on **0345 47 47 47**. This line is open 9am to 5pm, Monday to Friday until 24 July 1998 and offers an answerphone for out-of-hours messages. You can ring the helpline with general enquiries (we cannot deal with detailed queries by telephone) and to order copies of the summary.

Copies of Higher Education for the 21st Century and Further Education for the New Millenium can be obtained from Prolog on 0845 602 2260.

Participation in Learning

Higher Education

In 1996/97, 2.8 million students were educated in universities and higher education colleges (including the Open University) at a total estimated cost (including student support) of £7.4 billion. It is planned to spend around £7.6 billion in the 1997-98 financial year.

Trends and Features

- Full-time student numbers increased by 71 per cent between 1989/90 and 1996/97.

- One in three (33 per cent) of young people now enter higher education compared with one in six (17 per cent) in 1989/90.

- Almost two thirds of higher education students are mature students. Indeed, the number of mature entrants now exceeds the number of 18 to 21 year olds starting in higher education.

- Part-timers comprise just over a third of all higher education students.

- Female students now account for over 50 per cent of all higher education students.

- Students from less affluent family backgrounds continue to be under-represented in higher education.

Further Education

Of the 3.8 million students on further education courses in further education colleges, 1 million were on full-time courses, 900,000 on part-time evening only courses and 1.9 million on part-time day courses. The provisional cost of further education in 1996-97 was £3.15 billion. The planned cost for 1997-98 is £3.14 billion.

Trends and Features

- Over 70 per cent of full-time students in further education are under 21 years of age.

- Over 75 per cent of part-time further education students are over 25 years old.

- In November 1996:

  - 36 per cent of all 16 to 18 year olds were taking further education courses;

  - 12 per cent of all 19 to 20 year olds were taking further education courses, split fairly evenly between full-time and part-time courses;

  - 1.1 million people aged 25 and over were taking part-time further education courses (5 per cent of the total population aged 25 to 59).

Adult Education

In November 1996 there were over 1.2 million enrolments on adult education courses maintained, assisted, or contracted out by local education authorities in England.

Trends and Features

- Women accounted for 75 per cent.

- 679,000 (55 per cent) enrolments were for evening courses, or courses taught by distance or open learning.

- 51 per cent of all course enrolments were for physical education, sports and fitness or practical crafts and skills.

- One third of all adult education courses in LEA-maintained institutions were funded through the Further Education Funding Council (FEFC).

- FEFC-funded courses were mainly vocational (office/business and other vocational) or basic education.

- 72 per cent of all enrolments were on non-Schedule 2 courses, ie leisure and recreational courses which do not generally lead to a qualification.

Training delivered by TECs

In the academic year 1996/97, there were 305,900 starts in work-based training for young people (Modern Apprenticeships and Youth Training). The number of starts in Training for Work was 212,700. Planned expenditure for work-based training and Training for Work in 1997-98 is £751 million and £424 million respectively.

Trends and Features

- The total number of trainees participating in work-based training for young people has risen by a third since 1991-92. Over a third are now joining Modern Apprenticeships. Almost a third are aged over 18 on joining.

- Almost 50 per cent of those participating in Youth Training and Modern Apprenticeships are female.

- The number of people participating in Training for Work in 1996-97 was 216,300, considerably lower than the 290,700 in 1993-94, the first year of the programme.

- Around 30 per cent of those participating had been unemployed for two years or more when they joined; up from 20 per cent in 1993-94.

Employer-Funded Training

Employers make the biggest financial contribution to learning at work. In 1993 (the most recent comprehensive figures), the cost of training courses and supervised on-the-job training to employers of ten or more was £10.6 billion. While the vast majority of employers with ten or more employees provide some training, there are distinct patterns to this provision.

Trends and Features

- 82 per cent of employers with 25 plus employees have provided some off-the-job training over the last 12 months.

- But the employers provided this training for less than half of their workforce.

- Younger employees are more likely than older employees to receive job-related training.

- Employees in professional occupations are more likely than others to receive training.

- Employees who have good educational qualifications are more likely than those with no qualifications to receive job-related training.

- Training is less likely in smaller firms than larger firms.

- Formal training is much less likely in the very smallest of firms, with less than 25 employees.

The National Adult Learning Survey 1997[1]

The National Adult Learning Survey is the most comprehensive national survey of adult learning that has ever been undertaken. It involved interviews with a random sample of over 5,500 adults in England and Wales aged 16 to 69 in spring 1997. Respondents were asked about any learning they had done in the previous three years.

Non-Learners

Those respondents who indicated they had not done any learning in the past three years were classified as 'non-learners'.

Features

- Considerably more women than men were non-learners.

- The mean age of non-learners (48.6 years) was older than that of learners (39.7 years).

- Less than four in ten were in employment.

- Nearly a quarter were looking after family or home.

- Non-learners were mainly in: craft and related occupations (18 per cent); plant and machine operatives (17 per cent); clerical and secretarial (14%); personnel and protective services (12 per cent); and sales (10 per cent).

[1] The report of the National Adult Learning Survey 1997 is available from Prolog (tel: 0845 602 2260, fax: 0845 603 3360). Please quote reference NALS 97.

- Nearly two-thirds of non-learners were in the lower socio-economic groupings: skilled manual (29 per cent); partly skilled (24 per cent); and unskilled (11 per cent).

- About eight in ten left school aged 16 or less.

- Six in ten had obtained no qualification by the time they left full-time education.

- Only six per cent had received guidance about learning opportunities.

- Eight in ten said they were unlikely to do any future vocational or non-vocational learning.

- A high proportion had negative or neutral attitudes to learning.

- Half said nothing would encourage them to do some learning.

- A minority said they might be encouraged to do learning if available courses were different (12 per cent), or if their employment situation was different (12 per cent).

Vocational Learners

Those respondents who had left full time education and who indicated they had done some learning related to their current or future job during the past three years were classified as 'vocational learners'. Their learning could have been either in formal taught learning, or it could have been informal on-the-job learning, or other non-taught learning.

Features

- Over two-thirds of those who had left full-time education were vocational learners.

- Over eight in ten were in paid work.

- Only six per cent were unemployed and eight per cent looking after family or home.

- There were more men (56 per cent) than women (44 per cent).

- Over half of vocational learners were aged 20-39 years; just under a quarter were aged 40-49; over two in ten were aged 50 plus.

- Nearly four in ten vocational learners were in managerial, professional or associate professional occupations.

- Over nine in ten of all workers in professional or associate professional occupations were vocational learners.

- Over eight in ten of all workers in managerial occupations were vocational learners.

- A third lived in a household with a partner, but no child under 18; a third lived in a household with a partner and a child under 18.

- Only four per cent of vocational learners were single parents with a child under 18.

- The longer people stayed in full-time education, the more likely they were to be vocational learners.

- Nearly nine in ten of those leaving at 21 plus years were vocational learners.

Learners (Vocational and Leisure)

Those respondents who had left full-time education and who indicated they had done some learning of any type in the past three years, including learning for leisure activities, were classified as 'learners'.

Features

- Nearly three-quarters of those who had left full-time education were learners.

- Over eight in ten of all adults who had left full-time education and were under 40 years of age were learners.

- Over three-quarters were in paid work.

- Only eight per cent were looking after family or home and only five per cent were unemployed and available for work.

- Over two-thirds of partly skilled workers were learners.

- Half of all unskilled workers were learners.

- The higher the qualification obtained on leaving school, the more likely they were to be learners.

Printed in the UK for The Stationery Office Limited on behalf of the
Controller of Her Majesty's Stationery Office
Dd 5067955, 2/98, 61743, Job No 40996